LaDonna Harris

American Indian Lives

LaDonna Harris:
A Comanche Life

By LaDonna Harris / Edited by H. Henrietta Stockel

University of Nebraska Press, Lincoln and London

© 2000 by the
University of
Nebraska Press
All rights reserved
Manufactured in
the United States of
America ⊗
Library of Congress
Cataloging-in-
Publication Data
Harris, LaDonna.
LaDonna Harris : a
Comanche life / by
LaDonna Harris ;
edited by H. Henrietta
Stockel. p. cm.
—(American Indian
lives) Includes
bibliographical
references and index.
ISBN 0-8032-2396-X
(cl: alk. paper)
1. Harris, LaDonna.
2. Comanche
Indians Biography.
3. Indians of North
America—Govern-
ment relations
—1934—
4. Oklahoma
Biography. I. Stockel,
H. Henrietta, 1938— .
II. Title. III. Series.
E99.C85H284 2000
978.004'9745'0092—
dc21 [B]
99-38238 CIP

I filter everything through Comanche values.

LaDonna Harris

CONTENTS

List of Illustrations ix

Preface xi

Introduction xxiii

1. Where I Came From 1

2. A Comanche Girlhood 13

3. Learning, Loving, and Living 29

4. Politics and Partnership 43

5. In the Capital 65

6. Washington DC Insiders 83

7. Activism 99

8. Spreading Wings 109

Epilogue: A Continuing Mission 117

Notes 127

Index 145

Illustrations

MAP

The Oklahoma of LaDonna Harris xxviii

PHOTOGRAPHS

Following page 72

1. John and Wick-kie Tabbytite, 1956
2. LaDonna Harris, ca. 1945–46
3. Fred and LaDonna Harris on their wedding day, 1949
4. Grandmother Wick-kie, mother Lily, LaDonna, and daughter Kathryn, 1950
5. Kathryn, Fred, and LaDonna on the campaign trail, 1964
6. LaDonna campaigning for Fred, 1964
7. The Harris family, 1967
8. Fred and LaDonna, 1967
9. Fred and LaDonna during Hubert Humphrey's presidential campaign, 1968
10. LaDonna Harris, ca. 1974–75
11. LaDonna, campaigning for Fred, 1975
12. Fred and LaDonna at Taos Pueblo, 1978
13. LaDonna Harris, 1997

PREFACE

In late 1996 I approached LaDonna Harris to discuss my idea of writing a book about her. She agreed, not hesitating for a moment, and we were suddenly under way.

Friends for years, we lived only a few miles apart in New Mexico, and our mutual interests brought us together frequently. We both participated in New Mexico's Indian activities, she on one level and I on another. As a cofounder of the Albuquerque Indian Center, I was often invited to civic events, art gallery openings, and other ceremonies honoring Native Americans that LaDonna also attended, and we'd visit and laugh and catch each other up on our comings and goings. Then, too, there was always the neighborhood grocery store that brought us together.

These brief get-togethers built our friendship slowly and steadily. LaDonna knew me as a writer and western historian, with published books about Geronimo's people — the Chiricahua Apaches — and articles on the American West and Southwest. When I worked for the University

of New Mexico's Health Sciences Center library, building a database of Native American health history, LaDonna and I would compare notes on the historical medical conditions of the Comanches, she from the "insider's" point of view—conveying the oral history she learned in her family—and I from the academic observer's position. At one point I offered her the Native American health history database to place on INDIANet, her online subscription service for the nation's Indian tribes. At first she couldn't believe someone would offer her something for free, but after a meeting or two with the personnel involved in creating the database, she was convinced.

Inevitably, we also talked about our mutual friends and acquaintances in Cotton and Caddo Counties in southwestern Oklahoma. We usually had quite a few topics to discuss, for something was always happening among the Comanches and Chiricahua Apaches who live in that area. The people, the powwows, the Comanche fair, and the yearly celebration of the Chiricahuas' freedom were our favorite subjects. And we had Fort Sill in common—also in that part of Oklahoma. My visits to the fort to research the Chiricahuas' twenty years of confinement there and LaDonna's memories of her grandparents' and other Comanches' associations with Fort Sill served as another common denominator between us. Our talks usually ended with an invitation from LaDonna to visit her home and have a drink with her or a swim in the pool. But I never had the time, it seemed, to take advantage of the offers. Still, the invitations kept coming, both verbal and written, and so I felt comfortable proposing that together we write her biography.

LaDonna is one of the foremost American Indian women activists in the country. Though articles about her have appeared in local and regional publications from time to time, and a short biography was published not too long ago, no in-depth account of her life has ever been done. Little did I know when I mentioned the possibility of our joint endeavor that I would not be *the* writer of the record either. LaDonna has always spoken for herself, and this book was to be no different. Consequently, I became her editor, not her biographer.

At a time in American history when Indian women are being heard as never before, LaDonna belongs on center stage. Her voice echoes throughout Indian country, which is the length and breadth of America. She is admired, respected, and held in deference by non-Indians and Indians alike. Her achievements extend from her Comanche grandparents' farm in Walters, Oklahoma, to the White House in Washington DC. As a young woman she was content at first to reflect and admire her husband's accomplishments—Fred R. Harris was an Oklahoma state senator, then a U.S. senator, and lastly a candidate for president of the United States—and to be a mother to their three children. But along the way, the power of her Comanche heritage—she is descended from the brilliant orator and leader, Ten Bears—would not be denied, and she became restless. She strongly felt the need to become an individual in her own right, not to compete with Fred or usurp his spotlight but to share it as an equal partner. And so her long career as an Indian activist became a reality.

To succeed, LaDonna had to overcome her fear of speaking out, particularly in mixed ethnic groups. Growing up in Walters, Oklahoma, among Comanche friends and relatives, she was often protected from interacting with strangers, and so she was shy and, as she says, stoic. As time went on, her grammar school and high school friends were white, and her first boyfriend was white. But these friendships were different from, say, addressing the Junior League of Lawton, Oklahoma, who were strangers and judgmental. She failed their test and was not accepted for membership, and so she joined another civic group, one that was more accepting of diversity. She continued to persevere in her attempt to create herself and, in her living room, started Oklahomans for Indian Opportunity, a small group of activists that grew into a national organization—Americans for Indian Opportunity (AIO). When she and Fred lived in Washington DC, she met people from all walks of life and was welcomed into the Oval Office by President Lyndon B. Johnson. Yet she never forgot her Comanche upbringing, her first language, her grandparents, and what it means to be a Comanche woman. To this day she calls upon Comanche values to shape the way she lives her life.

My series of interviews with LaDonna Harris lasted more than a year and also included conversations with her daughters, Kathryn and Laura, and her ex-husband, Fred R. Harris. The only family member left out was her son, Byron, and that unfortunate omission was due to geographic factors that I couldn't overcome. Nevertheless, from the outset this book was destined to focus on LaDonna Harris only. By definition, that left everybody else out of the spotlight, but they all stood by just in case I needed editorial clarification. Most of the interviews were conducted in the AIO office, a compact structure in LaDonna's complex of buildings on the Santa Ana Reservation. She and her four-woman American Indian staff move easily between the office and her house, a distance of less than fifteen feet. It was sometimes necessary to step over Crazy Horse, a mellow long-legged dog that LaDonna adopted from a local animal shelter. Naturally, Crazy Horse has open access to everything. A resident cat ("came with the house") appears every now and then. Santa Ana Pueblo is located about twenty miles north of Albuquerque, just west of the old town of Bernalillo and some distance from the nearest grocery stores and restaurants. Ordinarily, one of AIO's staff members may be dispatched at noon to pick up some take-out food, sometimes down the road at the Santa Ana Star Casino or perhaps at a Chinese restaurant in Bernalillo. Lunch is then enjoyed in the kitchen of the house, and a short while later, it's back to work for everybody.

The outside of the renovated office is a combination of brick and weathered wood; the doors are painted a rustic red. It was once someone's home. Inside, a real business is in operation, with computers, printers, fax machines, an inverted glass bottle that dispenses spring water, desks, telephones, and a bookcase stuffed tight with tomes about Indian issues and the federal government. A small anteroom is set up with desks, two computers, and a framed photo of LaDonna. Two staffers work here, including daughter Laura Harris, and two work in the main room. The kitchen of this former residence contains the copy machine. Two bathrooms and a supply closet complete the layout through which LaDonna floats or stomps on any given day, depending on her mood, how tired she is, or how well she has been treated on the telephone by various callers.

For most of our interviews, LaDonna sat at a large, portable confer-
ence table covered with folders, opened and unopened mail, a telephone,
newspapers and clippings, and an occasional glass of water. A tall easel
stood to her left and always held a large white pad scrawled with various
colors, some psychedelic. Toward the last of our get-togethers, the table
was gone from the room, a sectional desk had been moved into its place,
and LaDonna reigned comfortably from a tall executive's chair, braced
by a cushion that helped her "achin'" back.

LaDonna is a commanding woman in size and personality and un-
selfconsciously fills the office and the house with her presence. During
the warmer months of our interviews, she dressed informally in blouses
and shorts. In winter, long pants and long sleeves were the rule. Some-
times she wore makeup, sometimes she didn't. From time to time our
interviews were cut short because she had a hair dresser's appointment,
or had to get ready for an evening affair, or had to take a lengthy long-
distance telephone call. Once, I remember, a masseur arrived, lugging
his portable table, and she apologized to me, saying she had a backache
and had to have the treatment. She invited me to stay and have a massage
myself, but I declined. LaDonna also suffers from asthma, and in the
early months of 1997, a serious upper respiratory infection, superimposed
on her chronic asthma, interrupted our interview schedule. She was abed
when I arrived, practically gasping for air, but sat up and shoved aside
the papers and magazines on the bedcover. "Sit down," she croaked, "and
let's get started." I left without another word.

Her closeness to nature became apparent as spring arrived. She hired
a gardener to tend the native bushes and other shrubs and trees that
surround the house, and she kept the office open to the elements. One
day a fierce storm came our way from the southwest. Most people would
have rushed around closing doors and windows before the downpour
arrived, but LaDonna opened wide the glass sliding door and stood
at the screen, getting sprayed with the raindrops and breathing in the
desert smell. Even the oppressive heat of the New Mexico summer was
tolerated. She brought out from storage a couple of tall free-standing
fans (there is no air conditioning in the office or the house) and made no

complaints as she sweated through a day's session with me. When the Hale-Bopp comet appeared in the night sky, she told me it was significant in that Comanches consider natural phenomena to be important to their tribal tradition, perspective, and understanding of cosmology.

Interviews were usually conducted inside, in the kitchen or living room, depending on the temperature that day and the condition of LaDonna's back. We often sat on hard chairs opposite each other across the kitchen table. While I faced the dining room and a framed oil painting of her beloved grandmother, she faced a kitchen island and a plaque imprinted with a saying by former Connecticut governor Lowell Weicker: "Nobody said it was going to be easy, and nobody lied." Other times we both sank into a pillow-filled living room sofa that curved around a coffee table. Watching over us was a framed photo of her grandmother in the same pose as in the oil painting. Other family photos occupied tables scattered around the living room.

Regardless of where we were on any given interview day, I frequently did not start recording immediately. Often LaDonna and I first shared news about mutual friends and familiar places in Oklahoma. From the start, our common background eliminated any artificial or real barriers that might have popped up along the way.

We decided during our first meeting that this book had to be an unconventional biography that would create its own structure and format as we went along. In our early, frank discussions about the project, LaDonna insisted on relating her life story in her own words and said, "Never mind the way other biographies or nonfiction works about American Indians have been written. My life is different, and I want this book to reflect that." I was excited and readily agreed, thinking about the Studs Terkel approach; but, that meant there had to be admonitions for all readers. Some may be disappointed because this book is not a history of twentieth-century Comanche life, an ethnographic study of Comanche women, or a full discussion of Comanche social and cultural complexities and academic interpretations of them. Instead, it is LaDonna's life story as she lived it and as it affected those she loved. She wanted to speak for herself—to have a conversation with readers at her

own pace as a Comanche woman—without having what she said filtered through the surrounding culture's multitudinous lenses and frameworks.

Respecting her wishes, at each interview I brought her up to date on what she had said during the last session. We had agreed to proceed chronologically, from her youth to the present day, and to adhere to a schedule of interviews that wouldn't be demanding. Although LaDonna was always so busy and often out of town, she was most accommodating of my schedule; only once or twice were our appointments postponed. We averaged about one interview every month or six weeks. When she received a typescript, she didn't read it immediately and edit and comment on it, but she set it aside for future reference. Occasionally, she passed the pages on to one of her grown children for their remarks. Periodically, her ex-husband, Fred, carried the text of an interview with him and returned it to her with his recommendations. She corrected only one interview.

We recognized that very few, if any, twentieth-century Indian women had documented their lives as we were doing. I had conducted interviews in the past among Chiricahua Apache women and included them as chapters or segments in books I had written, but never before had I participated in the type of biography/autobiography that we were developing. Neither had she. Fortunately LaDonna was easy to interview, and when I put our work together in the context of the ancient Indian tradition of storytelling, we proceeded with ease. At the start of each subsequent interview, I imagined LaDonna as an elder sitting around a Comanche campfire, a shawl drawn over her shoulders, and holding the attention of all listeners. As she related the story of her life, she would be interrupted with questions from someone in the circle—me. After responding, she would continue. Thus, our interviews were more than just questions and answers; they were reflections of her heritage.

Strong, secure, successful, opinionated, and independent, LaDonna feels she doesn't have to consider anyone else's judgment or measure of herself or her work. So, in writing this book, I deliberately took a back seat and decided that I would enter the work only with occasional comments and references in the endnotes. That is how it has remained,

with minimal exceptions. LaDonna's own words about her life, her loves, her emotions, and all of her experiences fill the pages, as do the narratives told to me by her family members.[1]

Some might say that LaDonna Harris is a very lucky woman. Others might see something more—a touch of predestination perhaps. She seemed always to be in the right place at the right time; helpful people appeared in her life whenever she needed assistance; and, she received enormous amounts of love from her relatives, her husband, and her children. She firmly believes in the Comanche way of life and attributes all of her blessings to following the traditions and practicing the values in all aspects of her life. Believe it or not, she has formed her own Comanche band, called the Toyahs. In the traditional language, "toyah" means mountain, and since there are a large number of Comanches in the Albuquerque area, and the city itself is at the foot of the Sangre de Cristo mountain range, the name Toyah seemed suitable. LaDonna and the other Toyahs identified six ideas they incorporated as their mission statement: The Toyah band of Comanches envisions a strong and healthy continuation of the Comanche peoples. To ensure this vision, the Toyah band will (1) be active citizens of the Comanche Nation; (2) keep informed of social, cultural, and political activities of the Comanche Nation; (3) help maintain and preserve Comanche culture and retain a historical perspective; (4) contribute to the future of the Comanche people; (5) provide a social setting to reinforce their identity, especially among their children; and (6) be informed voters in the Comanche Nation government.

Throughout this book LaDonna talks about being guided by the values she learned from her Comanche grandparents. One of these is the role of family, immediate and extended. In the Comanche way, you may rely on your family; you can trust your family; families make things work for the good of everyone. In true tribal genealogy, everyone is related to everyone else in one way or another, and so Comanches are available at all times for advice, assistance, or whatever the need requires. Tribal relatedness is not seen as dependency but as inter-dependency and mutual obligation, recognition of collective existence

and of group identity. Or, as LaDonna wrote in one of her publi-
cations, "being a good relative [means] basing the entire functioning
of the community on inclusive relational webs of mutual reciprocal
exchange obligations based on kinship principles. Relationships de-
lineate one's possible roles and, therefore, the responsibilities attached
to them."[2]

Another one of LaDonna's values is the sense of *ongoing community*
shared by all Comanches. "Traditionally," she wrote, "one became a
strong person in order to give back to the community. The commu-
nity nurtured you while you were becoming strong, and once this was
achieved, you looked for opportunities to give back to the commu-
nity. . . . The community provides a structure that is greater than an
individual, and within this unit are people who share your history, who
understand you, know you, know your grandparents, have seen you grow
up, love you. One highly prized characteristic within a tribe is the ability
to behave in a way that maintains these relationships, even through
disagreements. In order to be able to do this, one's focus must not be
on winning but on making the best decision for the community. Good
relationships are dependent on people feeling good about themselves,
which in turn creates strong persons who can contribute to the well-
being of the community."[3]

Sharing and respecting all persons also fall under LaDonna's umbrella
of values. In tribal understanding, love is profoundly related to respect
and involves valuing other people's vision of themselves. Politeness is a
vehicle of respect. Patience is another. LaDonna once wrote, "Sharing
is an institution in tribal societies. It is a prerequiste. It is not something
you do only if you have leftovers. In the tribal way, a person may be
poor in things but rich in relationships and the reciprocal exchange
obligations which cement those relationships."[4] Sharing a perspective,
for example, is an act of generosity in that one is bothering to share
one's perspective at all. Valuing differences in perspective is a gift of
potential insight, enabling the total picture to come into view. When
that happens, intellectual, emotional, and/or spiritual power is bestowed
upon the community. Careful readers of this book will connect these

values to the many circumstances and situations described by LaDonna in almost every chapter.

LaDonna's foremost role model has been her grandmother, a woman who was the equal of her husband. Mr. and Mrs. Tabbytite worked together to run an Oklahoma farm and to raise children and grandchildren. Wick-kie Tabbytite was the family member who spoke English best, who dealt freely with the Anglos in the surrounding culture, who was the family contact everyone admired.

LaDonna's mother, too, provided an example. As an independent woman, Lily Tabbytite was employed by the Indian Health Service in another town, lived on her own, and made her way in life without a husband constantly beside her.

Coupled with these lessons from two generations, LaDonna's own strong sense of herself as a Comanche woman has influenced the younger members of her immediate family. Daughter Kathryn Harris Tijerina, for example, states unequivocally that she is a Comanche woman, an identity she has carried proudly all her life. My first glimpse of Kathryn—several years ago when she was head of the Institute of American Indian Arts in Santa Fe—was of a young, blond, fair-skinned woman speaking fluent Comanche. It was during a celebration held to inaugurate the first exhibit at the adjacent Allan Houser Art Park. As part of the ceremonies, Kathryn welcomed everyone and then proceeded in the Comanche language to offer a prayer and ask for blessings.

Laura Harris is the darker-skinned daughter, the one who "looks Comanche," according to her father. Although Laura thinks she looks like the Harris side of the family, she also identifies herself as a Comanche. She wears her long, thick, black hair in a free-flowing style reminiscent of her Indian ancestors. She speaks the Comanche language but would like to become more fluent and so takes an informal class taught by an elder in Albuquerque. Laura is proud to say that she has hundreds of aunts and uncles all over America that are part of the extended Indian family that her mother created. Laura's child, Sam Fred, is the only Harris grandchild—so far.

LaDonna's former husband, Fred R. Harris, laughingly calls himself the "token white man" in the family. While married to LaDonna, Fred learned to speak the Comanche language and became the author of the tribe's constitution. To this day he remains the family's historian and can trace LaDonna's heritage back several generations to Ten Bears, who was active at the time when the Comanches roamed freely across the southern Plains. Harris has accomplished no small feat as family historian, given that the names of deceased Comanches were traditionally never mentioned again by tribal members.

Taken together, this family (to which the much-abused word *unique* could be applied in its full meaning), is an example of cross-cultural heritage that favors one side, the Comanche, yet is extraordinarily successful in accommodating the values of both. But I'll let LaDonna Harris tell you all about it, and about herself.

INTRODUCTION

Imagine a hundred or more happy, friendly, noisy people filling a large, tastefully furnished stone house on Indian land just upriver from Albuquerque, New Mexico. In the stillness of the high desert night their voices create a kind of music, a melody reminiscent of the Indian songs and conversations that used to fill this once-rarefied air, right here. A long, long time ago drums accompanied the singers, but nothing is pounding or pulsing at this particular party. Instead, the sound is made up of the whispering, chatting, laughing, and calling clamor of friends and strangers from varied walks of life. It is LaDonna Harris's sixty-fifth birthday party, and all of these folks, and more who haven't yet arrived, have been invited to enjoy the moment.

On that spectacular starry night, a long-legged, mixed-breed pooch by the name of Crazy Horse watched an army of automobiles file into the brick patio in front of the stone house. No one saw him; he was hiding between LaDonna's home and the building she uses as an office. But by starlight it was easy to tell that the vehicles ranged from battered old

pickups to new Mercedes Benzes, and everything in between. Another line of cars and trucks snaked beyond the patio out toward the local road that passes the Santa Ana Star Casino, an Indian-owned and operated success story about a mile and a half south. The neon lights of the huge casino sign blazed the night open. Beneath the sign, a marquee earlier in the evening announced, in fast-changing, blinking, yellow electric lights, the dates of the latest upcoming poker tournament, the current amounts in progressive jackpots, the time and temperature, and a personal message—"Happy Birthday LaDonna Harris."

LaDonna's two daughters, Kathryn and Laura, welcomed each guest at the front door and pointed the way to the dining room. On the large oblong table, a caterer had placed trays of delicious-looking finger foods and imported and domestic cheeses; in the adjacent kitchen a temporary bar was set up with a very small number of alcoholic beverages, mostly red wines, and a large supply of bottled mineral water and soft drinks. Every now and then more plastic cups and a fresh supply of ice in buckets appeared, as if by magic.

Somewhere in the sizable rooms, whose walls hold priceless Comanche artifacts and archival family photos, the celebrant herself floated among her many guests, not revealing her age. Dressed in one of the latest chic shades of green, LaDonna Harris would have been noticed in any group, anywhere. Tall, with short black hair, olive skin, and blue-green eyes, this Comanche woman has never had any trouble making an impression, not even as I have occasionally seen her—alone and without makeup in the nearby supermarket, squeezing the fruit.

LaDonna's circle of friends is expansive; ethnic background and occupation are meaningless in her public world, as was obvious at this bash. Proudly showing off their good upbringing, young American Indian men with long black hair slicked back in ponytails politely served plates of food to tribal elders who were talking shyly to each other as they rested on the sofa. Other Indians and non-Indians filed past the array on the table, selecting or rejecting this and that, smiling and talking amicably with the friend or stranger in front or behind. LaDonna hugged and kissed and was hugged and kissed in return by everyone, relatives and

friends, New Mexicans and Oklahomans, children who ran through the house and former college athletes who limped along on arthritic knees. Some of the guests could tat and some could sculpt. Some were artists and some were writers. Some of the politicians were in office and some in the room were their future opponents. Nonetheless, most mingled comfortably and waited for a signal to burst into the familiar "Happy Birthday to You."

That occasion came well into the evening, and after all the speeches were spoken and all the applause had ended, LaDonna made the appropriate thank-yous and expressed her appreciation. Not too much later the crowd thinned and finally was gone, the guests all driving off toward the interstate in their cars and trucks.

And when the stone house was empty at last, a tired and happy Comanche woman put out the lights and went to bed. Sleep came quickly, for the next year of her extraordinary life would begin in only a few hours.

LaDonna Harris

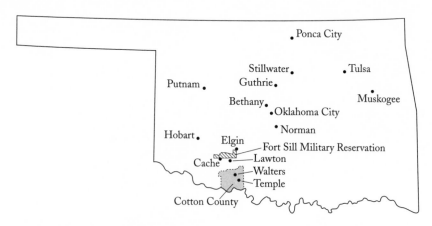

The Oklahoma of LaDonna Harris

WHERE I CAME FROM

I

I grew up surrounded by strong women.

The Tabbytite family farm in rural Walters, Oklahoma, was a good example of what U.S. senator Henry Laurens Dawes envisioned in the 1870s when the General Allotment Act that he sponsored began to take shape in Congress.[1] Through the Choctaw treaty of 1805, the government had begun the practice of reserving lands for certain Indian groups, but it wasn't until the mid-nineteenth century that members of Congress started debating seriously about extending the treaty provisions to all tribes. By 1874 Secretary of the Interior Columbus Delano had urged the adoption of homestead legislation for American Indians, and in 1877 his successor, Carl Schurz, recommended land allotments to heads of families on all reservations. In 1885 and 1886 President Grover Cleveland endorsed allotments in his annual message to Congress; he signed the legislation that became known as the Dawes Act the following year (8 February 1887). Among the primary provisions of the Dawes Act were the following four stipulations: 1) each family head would receive 160 acres; 80 acres were to be given to each single person over the age of eighteen and to each orphan under eighteen; and 40 acres were to be given to all other single persons under the age

2 WHERE I CAME FROM

of eighteen; 2) the land could not be "alienated" (sold) or "encumbered" (no liens could be placed on it) for twenty-five years; 3) Indian peoples had four years to make their selection of land, otherwise government officials would make the selection for them; and 4) citizenship would be granted to the allottees and to any other Native Americans who had adopted the white man's ways.[2]

Each individual in a family, regardless of age, was allotted land. When the time came for LaDonna Harris's grandparents to select land allotments in the late 1800s, John (which was not his Comanche first name but one that was given to him by the U.S. government for their rolls) and Wick-kie Tabbytite chose parcels of farmland that were across the road from one another. Not all their relatives made a similar choice, however.

~

Great-grandmother and others stayed right where they were, close to the Wichita Mountains. They didn't want to leave all that mountain medicine. A new outbreak of smallpox occurred at the time of the allotment, so the Comanche population decreased due to death, and that affected the number of allotments. It was interesting that the disease would occur at that particular time, but we also had an influx of people coming into the West. They brought their ailments with them. Our family went to Walters rather than stay nearer to Lawton.[3] Once we came to Walters we prospered. We had the best of all worlds—the farm and the creeks.

~

The Tabbytites (the surname means "the sun rays coming through the clouds" in Comanche) built their farm and reared their children—Frank, Clinton, and Lily—on Mrs. Tabbytite's allotment. Between 1900 and the middle 1930s, many children, grandchildren, cousins, and other relatives filled those 160 acres with running feet and happy laughter. Quite visible among them at any time was Lily Tabbytite's daughter, LaDonna.

~

The creek went down into Cache Creek and that's where Uncle Frank lived. When we'd go over there to visit my cousins, we'd have to cross where poor white people lived. Grandmother would cluck her tongue about how they didn't have yards and how they swept their trash out

with stick brooms. She'd comment how the little white kids always had runny noses. Sure, we'd get dirty during the day, but we were never *dirty* dirty because we always had to bathe. We cleaned up and washed up before every meal, and we had certain standards that were not kept up by most of our neighbors. I grew up surrounded by strong women. My great-grandmother's first husband was a Mexican captive and became a Comanche. I never knew anything about him in particular—she had about six or seven husbands. I remember her sitting with her cane, the empress of all her domain. Every man, woman, and child in our family respected that. It was the same with my grandmother, too, who assumed the same role. Both of them were matriarchs, great-grandmother and then grandmother. They were my role models. They assumed the responsibility of keeping the family together.[4]

~

One of the tried-and-true methods of solidifying the family was for all the relatives to get together on holidays, much as every other family did. However, the Tabbytite family was somewhat larger than most, given the Comanche cultural characteristic of extended families. Visits together weren't limited to holidays either, as LaDonna describes.

~

We never had a Christmas without going to great-grandmother's house. It made me close to all my great-aunts and great-uncles and all my cousins, who were like brothers and sisters. In the summer they all came to my grandmother's house and stayed with us—numbers of children. When my great-grandmother died, everybody came to grandmother's house, and she was the one who helped everybody. My grandmother was the one who kept the graves clean, and I would go with her. I would do some of the things that were recognized as the matriarch's role. I was always so proud to be with her. Going along with her would honor me—rub off—and the fact that I was with her and doing those things meant that she recognized something in me. To this day, people come up to me and cry. They remember my grandmother, and it ties me to them. They think of me as the legacy of my grandmother, and they hold me and cry.

Both grandparents had some memories of prereservation times. Grandmother was a child then and grew up under the tutelage of Quanah Parker.[5] Grandfather was born in the mountains around El Paso and had not been conditioned in what I call "colonial mentality." He wasn't submissive to authority in his heart and in his spirit. He had that spirit about him and although focused much on the old ways, he was still a contemporary man even though he didn't speak English. And Grandmother was a very contemporary woman in all aspects. She also believed in the old ways but knew its time had passed. I think Indians in general have shown great tenacity for that kind of change. Each of my grandparents had a touch of Indian boarding school but neither one of them followed set patterns. Papa [LaDonna's grandfather] ran away and Grandmother had to leave because of illness in her family; she had to take care of her uncle. Before she left, she had a taste of the colonial mentality, didn't get all of it, and wasn't brainwashed. They were still free spirits, but the next generation became total victims.

ROOTS

One story my grandmother told was about little people, like goblins, who had bows and arrows and had some effect on us. We were related to them. She would never go into detail about it and I never knew enough to ask Grandfather if we had a creation story—how we came to be—and so on.[6] I think the little people must have brought us to that place up north where we all separated out—the Utes, the Paiutes, the Shoshones, and us. You can envision that it was a big settlement and we weren't as nomadic, but once we drifted here, we became the Plains people. The way the elders told it, I got the impression that it took much longer in time than the historians indicated. I know that some of the people who came here were known as the Antelope Eaters [the Quahadas] and some were the Root Eaters [the Yamparikas]. My grandmother is from the Antelope Eaters and my grandfather is from the Root Eaters. There were a few other bands but I am not as familiar with the rest of them as I am with my own two bands. However, I know I am a direct descendant of Ten Bears.[7]

THE BATTLE OF ADOBE WALLS

In the late 1870s the indiscriminate slaughter of buffaloes by newcomers to Comanche country brought to a boiling point a furious resentment among the natives. In the months of December and January 1877–78, more than one thousand hides were taken on the Texas range. Buffalo hunters in the region believed they were performing a public service by removing the animals to allow cattle grazing. Their position was supported by Gen. Philip H. Sheridan, then in command of the United States Army's Southwestern Department. Sheridan believed the hunters were heroes and should be rewarded with bronze medals cast with a dead buffalo on one side and a discouraged Indian on the other. Said Sheridan, "They are destroying the Indians' commissary and it is a well-known fact that an Army losing its base of supplies is placed at a great disadvantage."[8] The general was correct from his point of view, which was to subdue the Comanches by any means necessary. On the other hand, the Comanches and their allies—the Cheyennes—were determined to rid their country of invaders who were killing off their food supply. And so the stage was set for a confrontation at Adobe Walls, a former trading post built in the 1840s near what is now Borger, Texas.

In June 1874 twenty-six buffalo hunters were lodged in the abandoned structure. The men had been working all night to repair a roof beam, and so they were still awake in the early morning hours when the Comanche and Cheyenne war party attacked.

~

The Root Eaters were among those who fought at Adobe Walls. When Papa [LaDonna Harris's grandfather] would tell us stories about the old days, he said he wanted us to know the story of Adobe Walls because his grandfather, who was a Spanish child when captured by the Comanches, participated in it. Back when he talked about it, we didn't know history—any part of it—and we had never heard of Adobe Walls. Papa told that a Comanche medicine man, Esa-tai, said that he had medicine that would stop bullets and that the people who believed in him should follow him to the west to wipe out all the European white people, and the Spanish. They recruited the Southern Cheyennes and the Arapahoes, but I can't remember offhand if the Kiowas were

there too. Papa particularly remembered the Cheyennes. Well, they rode west in high spirits. A lot of the younger men hadn't really had any war experience and were eager to go because they wanted to prove themselves. Papa said that when they got to Adobe Walls there was a mesa—a cliff—that they climbed on horseback. When they looked down into the valley below, they saw an adobe house that used to be an old farm. It had been deserted but at that time they saw some wagons and horses, and then they saw people. They decided to wait until morning to attack. Papa's grandfather thought they had better get the enemy's horses first, which was a common Comanche tactic. So, under cover of darkness he went down into the valley to where the horses were kept. He got hold of a horse's bridle and tried to cut the reins as long as he could. As he was crawling in the dark and following the line of the reins downward, all of a sudden he touched a face on the ground that was full of monstrous hair. Now, Comanches don't have body hair and don't have any facial hair to speak of, so it was the most frightening thing. He hadn't even heard this man breathe or could tell in any way that he was lying there. Just all of a sudden, he touched this hairy face. At first he thought it was an animal.

The sleeping buffalo hunter had put the reins of the horse under his head, knowing that the Comanches were in that area and might want to steal his horse. When this ancestor of mine got back to the warriors with the buffalo hunter's horse, he told the men how the people at the farmhouse were set up and warned them that there was a lot of protection down there. It was one of the times that he had proved himself. But the warriors didn't pay any attention to him because they thought he was being too cautious.

The next morning they all rode up on the mesa again and lined up. The Cheyenne chief was on horseback next to the medicine man Esa-tai with his son and he heard a shot, but he thought it was too far away to worry about. The bullet was from the long-range guns the buffalo hunters had and it hit an Indian in the leg and knocked him out of the saddle. The Cheyennes were angry because their man was hit and said that Esa-tai's medicine didn't work anymore. They left. Then the

Comanches and the other warriors stormed the farmhouse in waves. The whole intent was to just go forward into battle, but the long-range guns the buffalo hunters had was just something they weren't accustomed to. So many of them died that they just turned back, believing that the medicine man had lied to them.[9] They were so devastated.

That event was so devastating to their psyches because they had been all worked up and ready to do anything they could. They had the numbers, and it was the only time in my knowledge that the men from several tribes got together in a common cause. It was more of a psychological victory for the buffalo hunters and a psychological defeat for the warriors. I think it was because they believed so strongly in Esatai's medicine, and all medicine for that matter. How this medicine man showed them his medicine could resist bullets, and how he convinced that large a number of people to go out together when they weren't accustomed to being with each other—he had to do it in sign language because they didn't speak each other's languages—is amazing.

PALO DURO CANYON

The subsequent battle that occurred in Palo Duro Canyon that same year (September 1874) was a decisive victory for the military in that the Comanches were again psychologically defeated.[10] Both the Adobe Walls and the Palo Duro experience have remained in the Tabbytite family's memory. Although no hostility was obvious as LaDonna related the events to me, she clearly expressed some emotion.

~

The U.S. government could not have controlled us had they not had experience in the Civil War and learned from all those battles. Gen. [William Tecumseh] Sherman, who burned down Atlanta, came out here to figure out what to do about the Comanches because the government had been so unsuccessful in capturing the Plains Indians. One of his favorite strategies was slash and burn.

When the military pursued the Comanches, the Indians ran down into Palo Duro Canyon and hid. This was a tactic they used for years against the Spanish and it worked. It worked for a while against the

American military as well because the people would scatter; they had a prearranged place to meet when the danger was past. If women couldn't get away with their husbands, they took their children and hid in the bushes. Then the military gathered up whomever was left—usually older people, younger children, and women. They planned to take them back to the military post, but by the time they left the battle area, there would only be one or two cripples left, or orphaned children, or those who had gotten hurt in combat. The others knew how to sneak off, and as they did they stole the military's horses. Comanche women were just as fleet of foot and good at this as were the men. So, by the time the military got back to their post they had only a few captives and some horses.

When Sherman came out here, he said, "None of that." He was able to gather up a big segment of the Quahadas in Palo Duro Canyon by running their horses off the cliff. Hundreds of horses were piled up at the bottom. When the military had all the Quahadas where they wanted them, they burned everything the people had. It wasn't very much—tents and other possessions. Grandmother was there, as were her mother and the rest of the family. Sherman took the Quahadas back to Fort Sill, marched them from Palo Duro Canyon, which is right near Amarillo. Grandmother said it was miserable. They didn't have enough food, for one thing. It was the Comanche's Trail of Tears, so to speak. Very damaging and demoralizing, especially to see the army kill the horses that way. The horse had become a symbol of bravery and Comanche spirit. That battle really did break our backs. Then it was over. We were incarcerated at Fort Sill in 1874.

While they were prisoners, my great-grandfather—my grandfather's father—would sneak away into Texas and raid. He brought back things for the tribe to have, to restore some of their losses. My grandmother would tell the story, very dramatically, and it was so sad to hear her. She always mentioned relatives who had lost so much. Of course, horses were their wealth.

My grandson, Sam Fred, is nine years old and we are going to take him to Adobe Walls and Palo Duro Canyon and tell him the stories. We

must keep the memory alive, keep it going into the future. Sam Fred was named after the relative who participated in the battle of Adobe Walls. Ordinarily, we didn't give names of people who died to others, but it's different now. An elder said, "It's a good thing to remember those people. We should honor their names and carry them on because they were great warriors."

FORT SILL

Confinement to military reserves brought many changes to native cultures. At Fort Sill, for one example, some warriors joined military groups that were specifically created in order to keep the young men busy. In 1892 Troop L at Fort Sill was organized and commanded by Lt. Hugh L. Scott.[11] It consisted mostly of Kiowas with a few Apaches and Comanches. "The Indians made good soldiers," wrote Col. W. S. Nye, "Their average in marksmanship was high, their discipline good, and they were proud of the uniform."[12]

~

The young Comanche men around Fort Sill [in the late 1800s] were very restless on the reservation because they couldn't leave to go hunting or into battle to establish themselves. So, Lt. Hugh Scott and Sgt. Swett—Papa talked about them all the time—came up with the idea of taking these young men and creating an all-Indian troop as a way of keeping them occupied and giving them something to do.[13] It would also let the government know they had found some other use for the fort, as the government was closing down all the Indian forts. At that time there were no more Indian wars.

They took the young men and dressed them in elaborate military uniforms that looked like those worn by the Germans in World War I, even down to the sabers they carried. Their helmets had spikes on them, the jackets had gold braids, there were broad sashes around their waists, and the capes were blue on the outside and lined with a gold material. The army fancied the young men up and they took to it. Papa joined them. He said they gave all their commands in sign language because there were Apaches, Kiowas, and Comanches together, maybe even Cheyennes and Arapahoes. Papa liked it a lot. He got to ride a horse. My grandmother

said that when she saw them riding, and when the wind blew their capes back, they looked like yellow birds. They were so graceful, especially when they rode on the parade ground at Fort Sill.

QUANAH PARKER

After my grandfather left the army in 1897, he worked for Burk Burnett, who was the biggest cattle rancher in Texas.[14] Burk Burnett wanted to adopt my grandfather but Grandpa got into an accident—got knocked off a horse and hurt his leg, and it took a long time to heal. So his folks came and got him and took him home from Burnett's ranch. Still, the rancher stayed fond of my grandfather. Years later, when Papa went back to see him—Burnett was a very wealthy cattleman, the biggest in northern Texas—he bought Papa one of those big old hats—a Hoss Cartwright hat. Burnett knew Quanah Parker, and my grandmother just idolized Quanah. She always had the kindest things to say about him. We would go out to my great-aunt's and great-uncle's Nazarene church every now and then. Quanah Parker's surviving wife, To-pay, lived in the Cache area and she would go to church there, too, because she had been converted. Even though she kept the Indian values, she would go to church every Sunday.

We have a connection to the Parker family. My Aunt Rose said we had a Mexican Indian great-great-grandfather on the maternal side whose wife had been a captive. This woman could speak Spanish, English, and Comanche. When Quanah's mother, Cynthia, was taken away from the Comanches and sent back into Texas, Quanah stayed with this great-great-grandmother and her son. The boys became like brothers. When the army came to the Comanches after they were confined at Fort Sill, they asked, "Who's your chief?" Well, we didn't have just one chief at the time. We told them that and they said, "Well, we have to have somebody to work with." My great-great-grandmother was the interpreter, and by this time she had two grown sons. One was Quanah Parker and the other was her true son. She said to the military men, "My real son is a good man but he's hard-of-hearing, so why don't you work with Quanah Parker?" And that's how they chose him.

When Quanah became principal chief around 1875 he made a deal with the Texas ranchers to lease the Comanche lands to run their cattle.[15] The ranchers are the ones who built the big house with the stars on the roof for him near Cache, Oklahoma, at just about the turn of the century.[16] He always had tipis in the yard in front of the star house. Different family members used the tipis. When great-grandmother was ready to deliver a baby, she went there. My grandmother was actually born in a tipi in front of Quanah's star house.

Both Quanah and my great-uncle made money on those leases, and Quanah got that house, and my great-uncle became the primary stockholder and depositor of a bank around the same time. The bank furnished him a chair to sit in the window [of the bank] whenever he came into town. He had no children and lost all his money. I don't think the bank was robbed, but it went under in the early days of the Depression. Those were ill-gotten gains, anyway, and the whole matter was questionable because they got kickbacks from the ranchers who wanted to use the Comanche pastures. My grandfather, who was a Root Eater told me, "My folks never thought much of Quanah Parker. I know your grandmother was really close to him, but he acted too much like a white man for us. Even in the early days, he kept the best horses for himself when he was supposed to give them away and take what was left. He didn't do the right things." Grandpa was always critical of him, but I think he was a good leader. He fit that transition period—sensitive is what I mean.

And that's where I come from. Those are my folks. That's my heritage. That's what influences everything I do and how I do it.

A COMANCHE GIRLHOOD

2

I have to have the sun . . . feel the sky. . . . space is like a gift of wealth . . .

a sense of spirituality [that] may be strictly a Comanche value.

In 1910, the approximate year the Tabbytites were farming and starting their family, the entire population of Comanches was only 1,171 men, women, and children.[1] This was quite a difference from the estimated seven thousand calculated by Mooney in 1690.[2] Warfare, a low birth rate, and disease had dramatically reduced the population until well after the turn of the century.

The Tabbytite farm is south of Walters as far as one can go, because east Cache Creek and west Cache Creek come together there on the farm. Looking north one can usually see thunderclouds moving in, and a person will always feel the wind. It blows in Oklahoma all the time. Snow appears every four years or so, but rain and humidity are constant companions.

~

In the late 1930s from Papa's farm we could watch the rain clouds come, so as children my cousins and I were always ready for it. When we felt the first sprinkles, we would take off our clothes and run in the rain. Nothing smells like rain hitting the dirt, and it felt so fresh and clean. And then we'd find a little creek wash or gully and get in. We were always

barefooted in the summer. North of us was all that space and south of us was the creek, a small natural spring creek that flowed into the larger west Cache Creek. We would spend every weekend in that creek. Also to the north were timber and a place to play and get out of the heat. First we'd have breakfast, then run out the door. Maybe we'd wander around for a while and come back at lunch to grab some bread and bacon, put a slab of mustard on it and go back outside. One of the games we played was Nioka of the Jungle, a favorite game of Comanche kids I knew. It called for one individual, Nioka, to be in charge of an entire group of people who lived in the jungle. We pretended to hunt snakes, build huts, cook outdoors, and so forth. My aunt Rose Marie bossed us all the time just because she was nine months older than I was. She always was Nioka. My uncle lived nearby on the next allotment, about a mile down the road from us, and his three kids were always at our house. One was my older sister's age, one was my age, and then there was a little brother. And I had a little cousin who was so taken by World War II—he was a little-bitty guy who liked to stay in the creek by himself—that he would transform himself into a Japanese and would sneak around and watch us play. All of a sudden, he would come up and "kill" us. I can see him now. Somewhere he found clothes that looked like fatigues and made them into a Japanese costume. He wore the white headband of the Japanese, and I can't imagine why. Here we were playing Nioka of the Jungle, and he became a Japanese and punished us. Ah, but when it got too hot, we all just rolled into the creek.

If we saw cottonmouths in the creeks, we got out of there real fast. There were about five varieties of wild plums near the creek and possum grapes, as we called them. Raspberries and blueberries popped out in the spring, whole thickets of them that we ate in summer. We cut the grapevines and acted as if we were smoking them. We were very sophisticated.

Down at Cache Creek was a barn with an upstairs for grain storage and a shed for the cattle. Behind the barn was a pigsty with those little houses for the pigs. Nearby was a sharecropper's house that had been occupied, first by black people and then by whites. When they moved

off, we had migrant farmers and the crop changed from cotton to wheat. Papa cut the place in half and made one side as a breeding house for chickens and gave us the other side as a playhouse. It had a stove in it and there's where we would play dolls. Then when we got a little older, when our boy cousins came over we played cowboys. We made the house into a saloon and rode our horses right up to the door. When our other cousins came to visit, we all got together and stole watermelons from the people who lived down the road. Another of the games we played was that there was Spanish gold near Cache Creek; we made up all kinds of stories about that. Every waking hour we spent near the creek. So, that's how it was for us kids, day after day.

Papa always had cattle, milk cows, and all kinds of farm animals, but no sheep. Comanches didn't like sheep. They smelled bad. And no goats. Only cattle, horses, and pigs. Papa would holler for the cows to come in so he could do all the milking, and they listened to him. As children, our only obligation was to feed the chickens and turkeys. Papa drew the well water and poured it into a big tank. Then, depending on what size we were, we took a bucket of water to the chickens. And we'd have to water Grandmother's plants. She cultivated mimosa trees and zinnias—plants and shrubs that were hardy and could withstand the Oklahoma summer heat. My uncle dammed the creek so she would have water for her peach and apple orchards as well.[3]

Our big yard on the farm was fenced because Grandmother had to have grass and flower beds that went all around the house. The fence kept the chickens out so they couldn't get in and scratch or mess up the yard or the plants. But the cat could come in. Grandmother used to plow her garden with her horse and later on in life, when she wasn't as strong as she used to be, I would pull the plow to make the rows for her and help her plant. A lot of us helped, but I remember it because I spent more time with her. She always had a big garden with watermelons, cantaloupes, and cucumbers. Early in the morning we picked a cantaloupe and put it in a wet dishpan with a gunnysack over it. When we got through doing our chores—feeding the chickens and putting water in their troughs, or watering Grandmother's plants, or cleaning the globes of

the lamps—Papa would get a big knife and slice up the cantaloupe. We'd eat and eat and just be dirty. It was wonderful. Then we poured water on each other and cleaned up.

Grandmother made bread by working the dough and putting it in a big tin. I don't know what that container is called now, but you see it in a lot of Indian homes. The dough would rise and Grandmother made buns and loaves of bread. It lasted over a week and a half each time she baked. Coming home from school, we smelled it all the way from the bus stop.

We had a big old wood stove in the kitchen, and when it came time to iron our clothes the metal irons were heated on the stove. Though we didn't have running water, we had a sink with buckets of water nearby. Aunt Rose Marie and I heated the water on the stove and washed and dried the dishes. Also in the kitchen was a big round table, large enough for many people, with an oilcloth tablecloth on it. We cooked and fed everybody who came in the door. Of course, we finally got propane. Propane and rural electric changed our lives. After we went to propane, Grandmother had a stove put in the pantry. Well, it was more than a pantry but was built as one. It was a walk-in and was an extension to the kitchen. Grandmother churned butter in there too. We traded cream, poultry, and eggs to the B & O Cash Store. Sears later bought them out. The fact that the store was located in Temple drew people from a hundred-mile radius to trade. Sears carried dry goods, farm equipment, gasoline, and general merchandise. We also traded produce and pecans in winter. We occasionally stayed at Grandmother's second house in Temple when we were trading.

All the Indian houses in Oklahoma looked the same. We had a cellar on the north side of the house. We also had a cinder-block cellar and an earthen cellar where we kept potatoes; it had to be cleaned out every once in a while because it would begin to smell bad. We kept our canned goods in the cellars. All around the place were tall, big old natural Oklahoma cedars for shade. There was also a row of shorter cedars north of the house to protect it from the wind. There was a sun porch on the west side of the house that had rows and rows of beds for sleeping. In the wintertime

windows went up on that porch and Grandmother would quilt out there. It was warm enough, particularly on the west side. Grandmother kept her washing machine (with a wringer) outside on the south porch.

Grandmother had a sewing machine also, so my sister, my aunt, and I were the best-dressed kids in school. She made all our clothes and they were so cute. My aunt Rose Marie and I had dresses that looked alike, but with just enough difference—the colors. I loved navy blue dresses and big sailor collars with a red bow and gold buttons in front. We always looked properly dressed and had good shoes for school. I can still hear my grandmother saying, "Now, polish your shoes. You aren't properly dressed until you have the entire look. It's not just having a nice dress and then wearing scrubby shoes, or holes in your socks." Someone asked me once where I acquired my taste in clothes, and I said from both my mother and my grandmother.

MOTHER

My mother set the standard years before, when she was the reigning flapper. I always thought she looked so beautiful because she dressed so well. She had excellent taste and was very beautiful. All her life she did things just a little bit differently. For example, as a youngster Mother boarded at the Fort Sill Indian School because the government demanded it, but she cried her eyes out.[4] You know, they didn't encourage us to go to public schools at that time. Grandmother grew tired of all her crying so she took her out of the Fort Sill school and put her in public school in Temple. That's why and when they bought the house there.

Mother's first husband had been a high school classmate at Temple—a white boy.[5] His name was Carl Evans. I know nothing about him other than he was from Temple and it was the first intermarriage outside the Comanche way. It was a big deal, believe me. Can you imagine how the folks in a little old town like Temple would react to that? She named my sister Billie Carl Evans. (I'm LaDonna Vita. My sister has always hated that I have a more beautiful name, and she always thought that Mother loved me better, but I always thought Mother loved her better.) Years later certain attitudes toward intermarriage had not changed. My

ex-husband Fred Harris's people were not overjoyed to have me in the family. They weren't sure of me, and vice versa. It went both ways.

But when Mother married and left sometime in the 1930s, the times were such that nobody would talk about anybody who had gone away. My uncle Frank's wife, a Kiowa woman, told us some things years later, but not very much. It never seemed appropriate to ask because the conversation never led into allowing a child to ask questions. We got the message that the questions should be appropriate to the subject being discussed, you know, and if my mother was never discussed, there could be no questions. The grown-ups never quite said it wasn't anybody's business, but they didn't have to do that. The message came through because the grown-ups let you know in other kinds of ways. It was just implied. If a child ignored all that and asked questions, it showed bad manners.

After Mother and Carl Evans were divorced; I don't remember the date; she had come back home.[6] Eventually she married my father—a white man named Donald Crawford, who was a big-time football player at Lawton. My mother met him when he played football in Temple with my uncle Frank and my great-uncle Bill. My grandmother went to the games and ran up and down following the football moves, dressed in her little dress and shawl, wearing her braids over her shoulders forward. It was a sight to see—her so excited—and she always followed OU football.

My family had lived at Grandmother's [other] house in Temple during the football season, just so the boys could play at Temple High School. I think they all quit before they graduated, but my mother met my father there and they married. I was born in the farmhouse in her bedroom, with a doctor from Temple in attendance.

When I was just a toddler, Mother went off to work for the Indian Health Service at Fort Sill, and my grandparents raised me. Leaving [home] to work in Lawton or Fort Sill was a big thing for us, something like Mother marrying a non-Indian. Apartments were furnished for the workers at the Fort Sill Indian Hospital and my family and I would go there occasionally to visit with my mother. It was against the rules, but I used to stay all night with her. Everybody else in the dorms would keep it a secret and look the other way. The women played with me and gave

me gifts. They were all dating military men at Fort Sill and having the time of their lives. My mother was an assistant dietician. She had started off as a "blue girl"—there were "blue girls" and "pink girls," and each had different responsibilities. Mother should have been the dietician, but she didn't have all the training, so she always had a white supervisor over her, but she did all the work—plan the meals for the hospital.

My sister Billie had my mother's room until her last two years in high school when she had a room in Temple. She never graduated—just went off and got married.

That's when my aunt Rose Marie went to Haskell for two years,[7] and I left the farm to stay with my sister Billie in Bethany.[8]

RELIGION AND DISCRIMINATION

There were two Indian mission churches in our area, the Northern Baptist in Cache and Brown Church outside of Walters.[9] My grandmother was the second Comanche to be converted to Christianity in the Northern Baptist and helped raise that church. My family is buried there. However, we went to Brown Church, and it's too bad that I don't remember it very well. What I do recall happened when I was about eleven years old. All the kids had joined the church but me, and I held out because the circuit rider minister preached against Papa and his peyote. All of those types were full of hell and brimstone and really didn't like Indians. But the regular minister and his wife, the Howes, were good white people who also had a farm at Walters. I remember Mrs. Howe had a little portable organ. She had learned the Comanche songs and wrote them out so she could sing along with us. She sang the way they sounded to her. Both of them helped us memorize little church verses and Bible verses and put on programs for us kids—Christmas, for example. We'd have Christmas Eve at the church, Christmas at the church and Christmas at the house. We all got gifts, oranges, and candies. When Mrs. Howe got older, one of the jobs I had to do was to pump her organ while she played. That was because she was a petite, fragile woman and it was too hard for her to manage alone. The Howes were good friends and really cared about us Comanches.

But the others! They would say and do things that were so ugly. It was hard for me to talk to Papa about it, but once I said, "Well, Papa, these people say all these bad things about you and it makes me feel awful. What do you think? It's Grandma's church. Why do I not like it?" He simply said, "It's good for her."

Grandmother rationalized that the old ways always worked until the message of Christ arrived and then none of the old ways worked anymore. She believed that not even the traditional medicine could cure the diseases after the Word arrived, and that's why she became a Christian. Her way of thinking was very practical, I thought, and made more sense to me than just Christianity by itself. Papa said Christianity was what she chose for her medicine, and it was good for her, and you had to respect other people. So they never had a real controversy over it. Papa thought if you don't respect other people's religion, you'll hurt them, but more importantly, you'll hurt yourself because it comes back to you. So, you should never mess with that. It's the Comanche way. Papa was so logical and so reasonable, but I questioned the whole thing. I hated the hell and brimstone; it just wasn't part of my life. Grandmother never said what was a sin or what wasn't. She never talked in those terms, just what was right and what was wrong. She was an ideal Christian but I think it was because she was more Comanche than Christian. Her Comanche values made her a good person, and she just happened to take up with Christianity.

Papa was understanding and why couldn't the ministers be the same? Why couldn't they let Papa be what he wanted to be? Enjoy his peyote?

I questioned their authority because I didn't believe in it. Something like that happened with the schools I attended. They made me feel so inadequate, and I knew it was wrong. Education should not be like that. I got the impression the schools were saying, "If you give up your Indianness and become educated like us — be like us — then you will be accepted in our society. And if you give up your Indian ways and not dance and not sing and do all those Comanche things, you'll become a Christian and be acceptable." But what I noticed was that it wasn't true. Indian people were not approved, although I was somewhat more approved

than others were. I was fair-skinned and had learned how to manipulate people to make them happy with me. Skin color was important. It made a difference between my aunt Rose Marie and me. She was darker, was less acknowledged by white society, and still has a horrible personality—she's mean—from all those bad experiences. She never got over them and still carries the pain around with her.

As I said before, I loved the old Comanches because they paid so much attention to me. I would just stand by them waiting for a hug. They called me Little Granddaughter or some other kinship name. I loved them because they loved me. The schools said something was wrong with them, the missionaries said something was wrong with them, so I rebelled and said something was wrong with the schools and the missionaries. I was about ten or eleven years old in the 1940s when I could logically start putting some things together about that.

Well, I was finally baptized, and that is what I was leading up to. Grandmother never pressured me on that matter but the other kids in my family did by always telling me that I was the only one in the whole church who wasn't baptized. Thank God it wasn't like the Nazarene church where they come and pray on you. Nothing like that, but I knew it would satisfy Grandmother to have me become a Christian, and I loved the Howe family. The fact that they were working with Indians and the Indians were their friends made a big difference to me in their attitude and how they treated us. So, one day I gave in. You know, I'm always ashamed that I gave in, because I didn't believe in it, and I didn't do right—was only satisfying what somebody else wanted, and that's not really me. Anyway, the creeks were muddy and pretty well dried up, so there wasn't enough water there to baptize me. The solution was a horse trough on the farm, and that's where I was baptized.

Except for the horrible anti-Indian message that came across, going to church wasn't a bad experience because I got to be with all my cousins and a whole bunch of relatives and friends who are still very dear to me from that experience. Religion was very painful for me. Of all the discrimination that I encountered in my youth, Christianity was the worst. I was so disappointed that Christians would behave the way some

did. I still cry when I talk about it. I don't know where all my pain comes from, but their form of discrimination was worse than any I ever knew. That's why I felt so bad about being baptized. I didn't believe in it.[10]

[After hearing what some church people said about Indians], I would come home so hurt and ask my grandmother why they said those things. She answered, "Oh, they're just 'bless your hearts.' They don't know that they're being mean, and they don't know that they're being ugly." That always allowed me to have another perspective and feel sorry for them because they didn't know about Comanches. They didn't know the Comanche language, and they didn't know my grandparents and what valuable people they were.

I am thankful to my grandparents, particularly to my grandmother, who said that if people make me angry enough and I hold it inside, it doesn't allow me to think right. Then I wouldn't be able to define the problems, so I would be defeated. In other words, they have gotten control of me, and I have lost control of my spirit, so I should never allow anyone to make me that angry. And another thing, Grandmother put it in the context that those who would make me mad were ignorant.

All that negativity could have crippled me, had not my grandparents instilled a sense of self-worth in me. They sacrificed. You see so many people who are crippled by their anger. They are so angry that they're dysfunctional and turn to alcohol or other forms of self-destructive behavior, or they can't keep a job, or they don't continue their education. Discrimination doesn't allow people to see a way of overcoming it because those who are discriminated against are so torn up inside.

DEPRESSION AND WAR

When the Depression came it was so economically hard that my grandparents lost their house in Temple and lost a lot of money in crops. The Depression ate away at everyone, and my father's folks decided to move; they took off with the rest of the Okies to California. They had a bunch of kids. He had a twin sister named Alice and a brother named Travis. I met them only once when they visited my grandmother in Lawton, but when I was a teenager he used to write me and send me gifts, including

an identification bracelet that really lifted up my prestige in school. My father owned a dry cleaning shop somewhere in California. I wish I would have kept those letters, but I was busy with my life on the farm and with my grandparents, cousins, other relatives, and friends. I didn't think twice about stashing the letters in a drawer.

My grandparents were very creative even in those days [the 1940s] and they always had the newest things. For example, Papa bought the first car in Cotton County, and he had a radio in the living room.[11] My uncle Clinton built a wind charger so we could have electricity in the house, but the supply was erratic. It had a single blade and turned round and round in the Oklahoma winds. The generated power went to a battery in the house, so we could run the radio and, on occasion, have lights, although we could never use the lights when Papa wanted to hear the radio. We kids loved to listen to the "Lone Ranger," "Dick Tracy," and the "Green Hornet," but when Papa wanted to hear the news about World War II, we didn't have a chance. He always kept up with the war. He couldn't read or write, so when someone gave him a copy of *Look Magazine* or *Life Magazine* with all those published photos, he would ask me to sit down and answer his question: "Granddaughter, who are all those people?" I told him, and then he connected the news to the people in the photos. Papa loved Gen. Douglas MacArthur, and when he and President Harry Truman got into that fight, my grandfather just couldn't understand because he was such a strong Democrat. Papa liked Truman, but, of course, he worshipped Roosevelt. Nonetheless, he admired Truman's tenacity—staying in there and taking over—but he couldn't understand it all because he so admired the military.

MY FAMILY

All during his life my grandfather was less flexible than Grandmother was, but if you look at it in the whole, he was a very contemporary person. He even had two wives.[12] One was a Kiowa woman, and they all lived together at one time. Grandmother didn't talk about it, but we have some Kiowa relatives who carry the name Tabbytite. People still get confused when they read in the Lawton newspaper that Lily Tabbytite

from Anadarko was put in jail for something or other. But it's no wonder Papa attracted the women. He was a peyote man and very handsome. I remember that he kept his peyote in something like a chicken coop, but very small. We usually had from six to twelve peyote plants growing. I don't know where they came from, but they always seemed to be there and he told us kids over and over again to stay away from that place. We did. Papa usually dressed in khaki pants and always wore a nice-looking shirt with a kerchief around his neck. He wore earrings when he was younger but kept his braids. He wore a big old tall hat—a Hoss Cartwright hat. And he was meticulous. How he hated flies! Most country people live with flies and it doesn't seem to bother them, but we never had a fly in our house. I hate them too. My children tease me, but I tell them, "Boy, if you grew up with Papa, you would understand me." He carried a fly swatter around indoors and would go after every fly that came in the house. He hollered at us, or cussed at us kids if we held the screen door open too long in getting in or out. "You're letting the flies in," he'd say in Comanche. Then, "Goddammit!" He'd cuss in English and yell in Comanche. We had to be sure to close the screen door and to close the gate to the yard because he didn't want the chickens messing on the grass and didn't want the cows coming around. I can't blame him. Papa farmed a feed crop and would let the cows in only to eat the roughage; they got their water in the creek. All in all, there were four major gates that we had to make sure we shut. And we were careful to do it all the time because we didn't want him hollering at us. He never did anything to us but he made great threats. We all respected him enough to want him to be pleased with us, so we always listened to him.

Uncle Clinton, who occasionally lived with us, was my favorite. His room was off the kitchen and he had one of those record players you had to crank to get going. It was in an elegant box and complemented the fine furniture he bought for his room. Every time he married (and it was quite often—our family has a reputation . . .) he brought his new wife to stay on the farm for a while until he got another job or whatever it was that brought him home. I have a lot of cousins by him and his wife, Bertha. When he'd come home, he was always dressed so fine. He

brought back jazz records, so I grew up with Cab Calloway and all those jazz musicians. He played them all the time, such a dandy man. Then he'd go off and come back around again. He worked during the war [World War II] at Douglas Aircraft in Kansas City, and then I think he worked in Oklahoma City. He was too young for World War I and too old for World War II, I think. Well, he might have been the right age for World War II, but he was working in a defense factory, and I don't think he would have passed the physical, anyway. Uncle Clinton always sent me special things, and paid attention to me. He was our person who was adventurous and went way outside the community.[13] That bedroom was considered Clinton's room whether he was there or not, but at different times, as we kids got older, we could stay in that room.

And speaking of rooms, my uncle Lester had Clinton's room when Clinton wasn't around. Lester's nickname was Handsome. He was soooo good looking. Uncle Clinton was debonair, but Lester was physically handsome. Everything about him was good looking. I remember that he hated school . . . didn't do well . . . probably was dyslexic. He would play hooky a lot and mess around town all day, then catch the school bus home. Or, he would be under the bridge waiting for us when the bus arrived and then walk home with us. My aunt Rose Marie, the tattler, said, "I'm going to tell on you, I'm going to tell on you." All the girls were madly in love with Lester, both in Temple and in Walters, but he went off to war in World War II, which was probably a good thing. Papa believed that taking pictures with a camera captured your spirit, so we only have pictures of Lester when he was very young and some when he went off to the military. Lester was stationed in Germany, and when he came home, he did what every other Indian boy did—drink and carouse. He never got a job and was later killed in a car accident.[14] Lester's death was such a trauma for Grandmother; she went into a very deep depressive state.

I loved my aunts and uncles—just loved adults. Grandmother had given Uncle Frank a piece of her 160-acre allotment, so he lived close to us and helped Papa with the farm. When Uncle Frank came to the house, I'd sit in his lap and listen to him and Papa talk about the crops,

or about anything. I remember him being a big, heavy-set man. If I got bored with their conversation, I'd kiss Uncle Frank and run off. That didn't happen often because I loved to listen to adults talk. Somehow I knew that if I never interrupted, they would let me stay around. I have always gotten along with older people.

INDEPENDENCE

Billie married sometime in the 1940s, and I baby-sat for her daughter while she worked in a war plant. I was in the eighth grade. The mail was delivered twice daily, so we would march five blocks to the box to pick it up. Sister was always anxious to hear from her husband, Ray, who was in Germany. Besides school and baby-sitting, there wasn't much else for me to do. When Ray came back home right in the middle of the school year, they just packed up and moved. He had decided to attend Cameron Community College in Lawton, so they just left.

Nobody talked to me about what I was going to do. I still have a problem with abandonment. I finished out the school year by staying with my great-aunt and great-uncle (he was a Nazarene preacher named Amos Coma). Their daughter Gloria married a Ponca Indian named Makes Cry, who was also in the armed services but in the Philippines. When I stayed with them over in Putnam—it's a school district and was not much of a town—I helped take care of the Makes Cry young boys. It turned out that I was very popular the next year in the ninth grade, maybe because I also was a soda jerk in the drugstore and got to know everybody. It was my first real job outside the home. I also fell in love for the first time. The young man was a champion basketball player and president of the school government club. He always traveled with two other boys—his groupies—so I was safe with all these guys. We spent our spare time just cruising around. It was quite different from life in Bethany where children weren't even allowed out.

Gloria's husband Albert Makes Cry came back from the war in the 1940s with a case of malaria and it just wasn't comfortable for me to be in their house anymore. Albert was sick, they were married, and I felt out of place being there. So, I stayed with my closest girlfriend at her

house most of the time. Her mother had a lady friend, a Mrs. Nix, who was older and had only one child. They had a strawberry farm with lots of property and they were wealthy. She took a liking to me and I knew how to behave with older people, so she invited me to stay with her and continue to go to school in Putnam. That sounded all right to me and I still had my closest friend. I spent most of the summer and the whole school year with them. Mr. Nix was so quiet and distant that I became a companion for Mrs. Nix. I can't really remember much about what it was like staying with them, but I recall that I didn't enjoy it because they were so different, white folks, and there was no hustle and bustle around. Fortunately I was dating, and they allowed me to go out, so I had a real great school life. I got involved in the school clubs and took part in a great many activities.

But, there I was in the tenth grade, just kind of taking care of myself. By that time, maybe in the middle 1940s, Grandmother was almost nonfunctional, and Rose Marie was still off in school. Sister was going to school in Lawton, and Mother was still working in the hospital. There were no kids on the farm at that moment. I would catch a bus occasionally to visit my mother, and she always had a bunch of new clothes for me and would give me money. My family let me make my own decisions at that time because everybody was so involved in their own lives. Well, I wasn't really happy with the Nixes, so I decided to come back home to Walters. I had really gained a lot of self-confidence in Putnam because I was the only Indian around and ran with all the popular kids, but it just wasn't working for me and I don't know exactly why.

A PATH

While growing up I always wanted to be a wife and mother with a nice house. That was my great desire. As I got older, it changed somewhat, but I was never particularly ambitious—never wanted to be a professional person. I probably was inhibited by the fact that I am dyslexic and didn't believe that I could go on to higher education because I was so impaired. I limited myself for a long time. I knew I was smart, but I knew I had to do things in roundabout ways, rather than in ways everybody else

did. That kept me from wanting to be a professional person. Secretaries weren't even in the Indian vocabulary. Just nurses and teachers. I became very ambitious through my husband, Fred Harris.

My first real boyfriend was the one I mentioned earlier. He was president of the senior class and probably led me to Fred Harris. When I left Putnam and moved back to Walters I immediately asked, "Who is the president of the senior class here?" My aunt said, "It's Freddie Harris, and we really like him." I saw him and said, "Gosh, he's so short." Along with that, Fred always had unruly hair. Well, I thought he was interesting because he was popular among the high school students. I started flirting with him, and he immediately flirted back. When he first got the nerve to talk to me, I was at a birthday party for a Kiowa-Comanche fellow who is now a Northern Baptist minister. At the time, my aunt and I were living together in a bedroom-kitchenette across the street from the school in Walters. We had a charge account at the grocery store, paid by my mother or grandmother. Fred came up to the apartment with another girl but flirted outrageously with me, and I sure liked the attention. Most everybody was going steady in those days, so there weren't too many boys left to pick from. The girl with Fred wasn't wearing his jacket, so he was available. My aunt and I went to the birthday party, and after a while a little cousin who had a speech impediment ran inside and said, "Madonna, Madonna, Fred R. Harris is outside and he wants to see you. He just wants you to talk to him out there."

I walked outside and there he was with a whole carload of boys. He asked if he could take me home after the party, and I refused because of the friends with him. But I agreed to meet him at a juke joint. When I told my aunt, she acted like she had great standards and said, "On the first date? That's not right." I knew what was coming. She was the one who always tattled to my grandmother about me, particularly if I rolled down my long stockings to look stylish. Well, I invited her to join us, to make it a group, and she did.

Fred walked me home from the juke joint and that's how we got started.

3 LEARNING, LOVING, AND LIVING

My sister just knew I had married below myself.

Fred was coming around our apartment, and I learned that he was very interested in boxing; he had boxed before I met him. On dates during the latter part of my senior year in Walters high school we borrowed Fred's Dad's car and went to Lawton to watch my aunt's boyfriend box. At the time, Fort Sill had a big Indian boxing team who were mostly Comanches.

Fred was already at the University of Oklahoma, in Norman, and he and I would meet at his folks' house. I caught the bus from Walters to Lawton and Mother drove me out to his house, north of Lawton, a place called Porter Hill. He caught the bus from Norman, or would hitchhike, and we would spend the weekend together, going to movies, or taking his sisters out—innocent things. On Sunday evenings, he dropped me off and caught the bus back to Norman. Then Mother either drove me home or put me on the bus in Lawton. By that time she had bought a house in Lawton. When I look back on it, I wonder if anybody else grew up like this.

I always looked so mature for my age because I had fully developed bosoms. When I was sixteen years old, I could get into places to dance, like Fort Sill, so I'd take my blond friend, Floyce, and Fred and we'd go dancing. My aunt Rose Marie brought her boyfriend, we picked up my mother and her boyfriend, and added my uncle. He was so much older than Floyce, but he'd be her partner. Fort Sill attracted all the big names because they had two or three big old dance halls. Sometimes we stayed overnight at my sister's house—a Quonset hut—and sometimes we drove all the way back.

We did some really goofy things. I remember I wanted to smoke, and so I hung around my great-aunt, who was considered quite wicked because she already had had about four husbands. She let us do everything we wanted. We smoked there. Once we went out with my sister, brother-in-law, and my mother—it was kind of interesting that I could double date with my mother—and a bunch of others to a bar. I took out a cigarette. Now, nobody told me I couldn't smoke. My mother smoked two cigarettes when she got home from work, watched television, and relaxed. Well, when I started smoking this cigarette, my sister laughed. Of course I didn't inhale. I was just blowing smoke. My sister said, "I wish you could see how silly you look." I quit right there, even though everybody else smoked. In my senior year of high school, people came over to my apartment to smoke and I got really tired of it. Not only did it smell up my room, but it could have affected my relationship with the landlady as well.

My sister was always more of a mother to me, but nobody ever told me what to do or what not to do. I was just like a loose leaf. Grandmother said, "I don't know what you're going through, so I can't tell you what's right or wrong. You have to set your own values and stay with them." It's interesting that I didn't go crazy. Several people younger than me were already dying of cirrhosis of the liver, and some of the young women were very promiscuous. I could have gone in all kinds of directions, but I credit my grandmother for giving me that advice.

There wasn't anyone to set really strict guidelines, barriers, or limitations on me. I had to make all my life's decisions on my own. I look

back and think that I could have gone any way at all, but somebody would always come along who would be interested and give me enough attention to keep me from going crazy. For example, great-aunts always told me how pretty I was. It would do something for me psychologically and keep me on track. They would never lecture me, but always gave me some self-confidence. Different people such as teachers would love me and give me more self-confidence. My history teacher, a Mrs. Mershon, whom nobody liked, was one of my favorites. I was doing poorly when she said, "I know you know the subject matter," so she passed me along even though I couldn't spell.

I loved history. I had found a book that stated American Indian cultures were way ahead of European cultures and were more sophisticated. We never learned enough about Latin America, though. I wanted to know more, and we never learned anything about Asian history. It was all European history. My education was so limited. My least favorite subject was spelling. I could never have been a secretary. In school, everybody wanted to elect me secretary of clubs, but I couldn't take notes worth a damn. I still can't.

I couldn't play an instrument and was too uncoordinated to be a drum major, so in my junior year I figured out a way with a friend to get into the football games by being flag girls. Then we could wear short dresses and boots and wave the flags around. It worked.

I also belonged to the library club, and the glee club, and worked on the school annual, the yearbook. I found out there were two high school sororities and wanted to get into the most popular one, so I manipulated a lot of people to do it. I am still in touch with the woman who helped me join that stupid little sorority. During the initiation I had to go out to the cemetery and stay for hours. Going steady with Fred also gave me some prestige in school. I was nominated for homecoming queen, and I'm sure I was the first Indian who was even suggested for that.

We went to Craterville Park on our senior class trip. It's a famous old Comanche site that we lost in some way during the land allotments. The owner at the time made an amusement park right there with Ferris wheels, swimming in the local reservoir, and many other things to do in

a carnival-like atmosphere. It was very special to go there from Walters, and I had been there several times when, as a child, we visited our relatives in Cache. When Fort Sill expanded to a missile site, the army took over Craterville Park, and it's under army control now. But back then, during our senior class trip, we drank a couple of bottles of beer on our way home. We stopped someplace and, darn, if Fred's cousin didn't see us and reported that we, and the agriculture teacher, who was one of our sponsors, were drinking beer. It caused so many problems. I lied for the teacher so he wouldn't get into trouble. He and his wife were good friends, and Fred was his protégé.

Fred won the Future Farmers of America speaking contest for the state. He had entered the speech contest with the topic "Can Our Earth Feed Its People?" He addressed overpopulation, erosion, and all those types of problems. Carl, that same ag teacher, and his wife invited me to go to Dallas to the regional to hear Fred. He won all the awards for Walters High. Well, Fred went on from the regional to the national and came out second. His speech was recorded, and someplace among my stored-away things is that old record. Fred was big in FFA, had a jacket, and I wore it. We were going steady.

He and his friend Dan Bigbee and someone else bought off-brand chickens and entered them into the state fair. One of the things that impressed me about him was all the ribbons he won at the state fair. Well, he bought these chickens and then put them in his sister's name and the names of other family members. As a chicken judge, he kept the best chicken for himself. They went from county to county judging chickens and entered them into county fairs. He judged which one was the best that he entered, and then he put the rest in his sister's name. It turned out that his sister won the prizes. None of his family was particularly interested, but he got written up in the *Walters Herald*. It so impressed me that he was smart enough to win all those boxes and boxes of ribbons.

Since I have mostly happy memories of those days, people tell me I block out the bad memories. In high school I was the stoic girl who didn't say very much but watched everybody. I studied people. You can

imagine how boring it was for my girlfriend Floyce and me, who were dating college students, but we managed to stay real active in school. When we went out to honkytonks, I was always afraid of the sheriff's office people. An Indian should always be wary. In later years, I told my children that if the police or the sheriff ever stopped them, to put their hands and feet up in the air and be very passive.[1]

Those were fun years, the most fun time I remember in school, but I still have nightmares about not passing school. I felt like I just faked my way through it, but I got my high school degree. I was so active in school that I had roles to play in graduation. I wasn't the valedictorian or the salutatorian, but I was one of the major speakers at the graduation ceremonies in the late 1940s. Fred was off at school, and Mother couldn't come down. I didn't have any of my family there for my graduation.

Right in the middle of the event, the tornado warning siren came on. Walters is located in tornado alley. We had been hit several times, so understandably people were shy. When the alarm went off several people got up, took their coats, and left. Others in the audience began to buzz, buzz, buzz and weren't paying proper attention to us. Sitting up on the stage, I could see all the nervous behavior. Then the audience just up and left and all the seats were empty with the exception of only four or five people still there when we paraded out of the auditorium, with the tornado siren still screaming. As I recall, that was the time Walters had its first major car accident. Cars ran into each other while people were trying to get to the tornado shelter.

MARRIAGE AND STARTING A FAMILY

Toward the end of high school, when I wanted to get married, my mother and sister and Fred's father all had fits. Mother saw me going to modeling school. I was their great white hope, I guess, or something like that. I was going to be her whatever-she-had-in-mind. Sister wanted me to go to school. She was convinced that I would marry below myself to this poor farm boy. I remember telling Fred's father about us before we were married. He said, "By God, I'm not going to support y'all." Fred answered him by saying, "You haven't supported me in the last five years,

and I don't expect you to start now." His father got angry because he was afraid Fred would have to drop out of school; that's what was hurting his feelings. On the other hand, Fred's mother was very caring, and she immediately said, "Oh, that will be wonderful." She started planning the wedding right away. My grandparents were also lenient. Their attitude was something like "whatever you want to do."

Well, Fred and I got married in 1949 right before high school was out. [The ceremony was at] the Baptist church, a little country church, right there at Porter Hill. I wore a white suit and a little white hat. I had planned to go back to OU with him but he decided I had to earn money for the both of us. So, I didn't go. I worked as a waitress in Walters and stayed there near my grandparents and his relatives. But right after we were married he went off to the wheat harvest because it was the fastest and biggest money he could make. I think he went as far as South Dakota and then came back. He had said he wouldn't continue to do that after we were married, but it paid so much.

Right after we were married we paid calls on our neighbors and relatives. I remember one in particular, a neighbor named Cecil, a prosperous Comanche farmer whom Fred had always liked. While we were there, Fred admired a picture of Scott Momaday's father that Cecil had. So, when we were ready to leave, Cecil's wife, Margaret, took the picture down off the wall and gave it to Fred. That's how we got that valuable item. It was valuable because of who it is.[2] When I lecture to groups, I say Comanches are never supposed to own anything they can't give away, because possessions are not necessary in the Comanche value system. If you admire my jewelry, for example, I should take it off and give it to you right then. However, I also admit, "Don't try it because I have been hanging out too long with white people. I've been acculturated."

We moved to Norman, right near the university, after Fred came back from the harvest that summer of 1949. He had an uncle and aunt in Norman who were World War II veterans and had two kids. We lived in a trailer house with these relatives and I baby-sat for his family. We had to go outside to use the bathroom and to shower.

I became pregnant soon afterward and was so ignorant about life and responsibilities that I can look back now and say I didn't know from shit. We were living on the money Fred's job brought in, his scholarship, and what little I could make babysitting. I went to an old country doctor. Marion Martin, M.D. was his full name. He gave me vitamins, took care of me, and said he would charge us fifty dollars for the whole thing. I just loved that doctor. Later on he was appointed rural doctor of the year, nationwide. He was such a kind and dear man. He had one bad eye. I'd come from Norman to Elgin, where he practiced, and stay with Fred's family so Dr. Martin could examine me. The doctor was only ten miles or so up the road from that house. Fred's mother had been a midwife who helped with many deliveries in her younger days. His mother was such a big help. She subscribed to the *Farm Home Delivery,* and we read it from cover to cover. Because we were pinching pennies, Fred's family gave us food from their garden, and chickens. I thought I'd never want to eat another chicken in my life when it was over. My mother bought us clothes, so I always had a nice appearance. Fred's mother and I decided I would have the baby at their home, and Dr. Martin agreed. He said, "You're a healthy girl and you're living close to Lawton, so if anything goes wrong, we'll take you right to the hospital."

Fred was just delightful. He read Dr. Spock to me, we took walks together, and he took a great interest in the whole thing. One time while I was pregnant we took an afternoon walk. It was winter, around Christmas of 1949, and we were so poor that we couldn't afford a Christmas tree. Well, we stole a little-bitty one from someone who was selling them. It was our first Christmas tree together.

I stayed with my in-laws for nearly the whole last month of the pregnancy. I didn't think of making a Comanche cradleboard because Fred's folks influenced me in the other direction, but the whole pregnancy was so much fun because Fred was so interested. His mother picked it right up and did mothering things. My own mother couldn't sew on a button. His mother just took over. She's a very strong woman, but she wasn't mean about doing it. We didn't know what gender the baby would be, but we got a little white bassinet, and my mother-in-law lined it all in

satin with ruffles and a skirt. The baby didn't have one thing that wasn't crocheted or embroidered, even her sheets — everything but her diapers. Fred's mother made her the most beautiful satin dresses and several sets of clothes.

On the day I started becoming uncomfortable, either January 11 or January 12, 1950, my mother-in-law walked me all the way from the house to Porter Hill, which was quite some distance, about a mile and a half. All the way back I had contractions, so when we got home she gave me a dose of castor oil. It worked. There was time to take a bath, wash my hair, and roll it up so I would be clean for the birth. Then we followed all the things the booklet told us to do.

Fred's mother set up the birthing place in the living room of their old farmhouse that was probably built in the late 1920s or 1930s. I felt like I was on stage and was giving a grand performance. By that time Fred's father and I were getting on really well. I became his favorite daughter, so to speak. When I lived with them, he wouldn't let me hang up clothes because the cord could wrap around the baby's neck. It was an old wives' tale he heard from his mother.

Damn if the baby didn't come during Fred's semester exams. I told him it was more important for him to make good grades, so he should stay where he was. He said, "As soon as I get out of here I'll borrow a car and come right down." I don't know how he got through his exams because he was so involved with the pregnancy. Well, Fred got to the house just after Kathryn was born. It was an easy delivery. Fred's mother and Dr. Martin gave me just a little whiff of ether once in a while and talked and talked to me. There I was, in this bed in the living room with Fred's father, his mother, and his younger sister with me. One of his other sisters stayed all night too. His father was fine for a while, really getting into the act and then, when I started hurting real bad, he went outside and sat in the pickup truck. I guess he was bored. At the end, only the doctor and Fred's mother were with me. When labor started, it was probably about two hours at the most.

She came out with blond hair, very little of it, on top of a big round head and a little neck. From my bed, I could see Dr. Martin and my

mother-in-law in the kitchen, washing the baby and dropping liquid into her eyes. When his exams were over, Fred borrowed a car from one of the senior class members and drove on down. When he arrived, there was a big celebration. He didn't have to go back soon so he stayed over the weekend. Everybody came the next day, Grandmother and Mother. I was still in the big bed. Women stayed in bed for seven days back then, but I was ready to run up and down the road by the next day. Dr. Martin wouldn't allow it, so I held forth like a queen. Everybody waited on me. It was just lovely. The only problem was that it was very painful for me to get her to start nursing because my breasts would harden up. But, I'm glad I did it anyway because it was very satisfying.

Fred came to Porter Hill another weekend, and by that time I was ready to go home. He was fussy and didn't want anyone touching the baby but his mother and me. Of course, I was sharing her with everyone. It gave me such joy to play with her, talk to her, hold her, and touch her, so I truly believed I should share her. Fred felt differently. He remembers when we caught the bus to go home and Kathryn was wearing a pink outfit. She looked so beautiful in a satin dress with puffed sleeves and shoes to match. An old grizzly man with a beard came over to us and said, "Oh, what a pretty baby." I held her up so he could talk to her and then he asked to hold her. I said, "Yes," and Fred got so mad.

KATHRYN

After Kathryn was about two years old, I babysat for other children whose parents worked. Kathryn was with me and she learned everything, was the quickest child I knew.[3] Walking, potty training, she was just a delight. We didn't have a car, but Kathryn had an old-fashioned European baby buggy. We wheeled her in it and went to the movies. When she got restless, I breast-fed her right there, in the dark theater. We'd take her to buy groceries and put them in the buggy with her. That was our mode of transportation in Norman, Oklahoma. We were still living in trailer houses and had rented one in the same park as Fred's aunt and uncle.

I remember when my sister came to visit us. By that time she had moved to New Mexico and wanted to see the baby, so she made the long trip. Well, the whole city of Norman at that time was inundated with rats. Us too. I hadn't bothered to tell her, because I just didn't think about it. But I had reported the rats to the housing authority, telling them we had a baby in the house. The man I spoke with said something awful like, "Why don't you feed them?" I was so incensed.

Our trailer house was partially furnished, and we had a little couch too. There was only a single set of springs for a bed, so we put boards across it and then got two single mattresses. After dinner I said to my sister, "We'll let you have the bed," and as we sat talking, she got a call at Fred's uncle's house (we didn't have a telephone). Her husband was checking on all of us and wanted to know how we were and what she thought of the baby. When she came back, we all went to bed, and I took the baby in with us for the night. The first thing that happened was that Sister sat down wrong on the bed and—kerplunk!—she fell. We had to settle her down. Later, we were sound asleep and all of a sudden we heard her scream. One of the rats had gotten in the house and jumped in her bed. Well, right then she just knew that I had married below myself. Fred chased the rat around the house and it finally went into the built-in cabinets. We could hear it gnawing inside the cabinet. The whole city of Norman finally went on a rat eradication program, not just because of us but because there were so many complaints.

When Kathryn was old enough, I sent her off to day nursery school, but I didn't like the woman who was in charge. I was probably over-protective, but she was so little. At first I fixed Shirley Temple curls for her, but when I started working I gave her a Buster Brown haircut. Anything else was too much trouble. I found a rural woman who had worked in day care and was taking care of three to four kids at any time in her old farmhouse. She picked them up in the morning and delivered them back home. It was ideal. I don't know how she made any money, but she did, and it was wonderful for the children. That farm woman took care of Kathryn for about four years. It was a wonderful arrangement.

LOVE AND WORK

Fred was still in school at the University of Oklahoma, working, and getting scholarships. A staff person at ou found me a job as a hostess at the faculty club. I seated people and made sure they were comfortable. They probably made the job for me because everybody liked Fred so well. It didn't pay much but was a great experience. Next, I went to work for the library in the periodicals section. I checked in all the periodicals at ou's main library and distributed them, and opened and distributed mail and whatever else there was to do. Generally, I just made myself useful to everybody, sort of a go-fer. I loved it. I told Fred that when the kids (we only had one at the time) got old enough, I was going to become a librarian. I loved being in the library with all those books. I guess it stemmed from my old high school days.

Well, then ou reorganized and did away with my job. I was devastated. It broke my heart to leave the library. But, ou's Center for Continuing Education hired me to take care of copying all those correspondence courses the school had. Nobody had been responsible for that job, so all the stencils were dirty. Nobody had retyped them. I cleaned up the stencils and did a wonderful job, even had my own little office. Also working there was a woman who wore her hair in a bun. She had so much energy even though she was very old. If I got all my work done early and when reading wouldn't satisfy me, I'd go right down the hall to her office and help her. She clipped periodicals, alumni news, and stories about famous Oklahomans and made files of them. When people wrote to the Continuing Ed department asking for information about a certain person, we had all they wanted.

My job was to staple the items into a folder and label them so we had them easily available. Previously, she'd had to do all the work herself, as well as answer the telephone, so I became invaluable to her. Administration let me do both these jobs but didn't increase my pay, and that was basically my working life during those times.

Other things were happening, though. The trailer courts were eventually torn down to expand ou's athletic activity. By then, most of the veterans had graduated anyway. In the early 1950s Fred, Kathryn, and I

moved into a big old house that was built in the 1930s or earlier. It housed a floral shop on the ground floor. The manager said we could either pay all our rent or work in the floral shop and help her. That would offset our rent payment. Our bedroom was a big old empty place. We fixed our bed and Kathryn's in there. Naturally, we had no furniture but we got a couch somewhere, and then Fred built a coffee table and two end tables out of plywood. We painted them up real nice.

By that time Fred was in law school at OU and was president of the League of Young Democrats. He and members of the League of Young Republicans had a radio show where they would comment on the state legislature's activities. We didn't think anyone but our mothers listened. Most of the other students in law school weren't married and would come over to our house to study with Fred. He was so smart that we always had a house full of students.

When Fred was an undergraduate, I had helped him study by reviewing the questions, asking questions, selecting questions. Many of the classes he took that he enjoyed the most he would share with me, especially in botany and geology. Part of his learning was to teach me and to share with me what he had learned. I almost felt as if I, too, had taken the course. For the botany class we had collected leaves together and I could distinguish which leaf was what. While he took geology, we drove around to look at the different ranges. Everything he learned, he shared with me. We didn't have very many friends, particularly in undergraduate school, so we had each other. It was different, though, in law school where we had a great many friends.

We always hoped there would be a funeral in Norman so we could work in the floral shop to pay off our rent. If that happened the owner would have to run around to make all the flower pieces. We were terrible. There were six or so boys living over the flower shop also. Fred and one of those boys planted all the bulbs for the owner, and they didn't come up. They planted them upside down! We didn't know what we were doing, obviously, but I loved working with the flowers and the plants. When the farm lady couldn't take care of Kathryn anymore, we were lucky in that a couple bought the house next door to the flower shop.

He was raising chinchillas, and she was raising fish in their retirement. They volunteered to take care of Kathryn because I was still working at Continuing Ed. Fred was still working too and was at the top of his class. He loved law school.

While Fred was at OU law school, there was a fight between the engineers and the lawyers. The engineers painted the law school black and the lawyers decided to retaliate. They cut the figure of an owl out of tin, got some paint, and painted it all over the engineering school. They almost got caught, but didn't. Instead, they were reported and the police came. The lawyers rushed off to our home. We were all hysterical, afraid the police would get us. They didn't. Fred told one of the journalists about the engineers, so it was written up in the newspaper. The lawyers finally paid those dumb engineers back.

[Although] I liked my job and I liked the people at OU, I remember two incidents that hurt my feelings so badly. One had to do with the dean of the law school, who came and talked with the law wives (our organization) and said that the law was a jealous mistress. He meant we had to give in to it. I hated the way he said it. Instead of saying that wives had to be partners and be supportive, it was just as if he told the students to forget their wives.

Another incident had to do with a black student. OU had just closed out their separate-but-equal education and had the first black law student. He was isolated from the rest of the class by a rope. Can you imagine? He was behind a rope. They finally did away with the rope, and then there were two black students. The law wives' organization gave Fred a scholarship, and they made me chairman of the Decorations Committee for the annual fund-raiser dance. I selected my committee: the two black women who were the wives of the black students.

Well, another woman and I were on the way to pick up one of these wives when I realized I had never before been in a black person's home. I was so ashamed of myself for even thinking it. I believed I had gotten rid of all prejudice and there I was, wondering what her house would look like because she was black. I was so mad at myself. What made it even worse was that I had gotten calls from the older women in our law

wives' organization saying that I shouldn't have her on the committee and should get rid of her. Of course I didn't, and made sure that both couples sat with Fred and me and our friends at the dance. I kept both women on the committee, but should have said more, should have acted out more, but I was too insecure to know how to react. I wasn't overly harassed about this because Fred was a top student in law school and had been a Phi Beta Kappa undergraduate. It meant quite a bit. Also, I never learned of anybody acting against me either, but I'm sure it was there. If they were that openly vulgar toward blacks, I'm sure there was something awful, like hatred, in their minds and hearts toward Indians. There were only five Indians or less in law school for some time.[4]

When Fred was in law school, I think I began to come into my own. He took such good notes that all the students would come to our house. I'd fix coffee and refreshments for them, but I wasn't a full partner then, not like I felt later after he got elected to the state senate. For a long time I felt inadequate because I didn't have the formal education, and then my dyslexia kept me from doing certain things I would have liked to have done. But it became less and less because I became more creative and found many activities. I think of those days as some of my happiest. We were poor as snakes. I never could cook anything because I didn't have the right ingredients, but I was very creative with hamburger meat. Between his scholarships and both of us working at very low-income jobs, we made it. Mother bought me clothes, Grandmother brought food every now and then, and Mother bought the baby the shoes, coats, and other necessities she had to have. We inched by. I never thought of those times as being hard because we did it together and it built a relationship that lasted for years.

POLITICS AND
PARTNERSHIP

4

They called us "Freddie and the Indian."

The political bug bit Fred R. Harris early in his life, when he was a student at
the University of Oklahoma's law school in the 1950s. To his credit, he fought
off this infection as long as he could, which was until his senior year. Then he
tried a run for the state legislature while he was still in law school. LaDonna
remembered it clearly, with amusement.

~

Fred had gotten another scholarship. He was working, I was working,
and he garnered up a car. He drove to Cotton County from Norman
every weekend to campaign. Three candidates were in the race, but one
died. Believe it or not, the dead man got enough votes to throw the
election into a runoff. We actually won the first time but then lost in the
runoff by about eight votes.

TROUBLE WITH OIL
When Fred was newly out of law school in the middle 1950s, Grand-
mother and Papa were still on the farm. When we visited them Adlai

Stevenson was running for president and, of course, being strong Democrats, they were supporting him.

Grandma said, "Fred, I just don't understand this offshore drilling. What does that mean? These people in parts of Oklahoma and Texas really are mad about that." Fred explained it to her. I remember those kinds of conversations because my grandparents were so inquisitive and wanted to know everything, all about the campaign and what had created problems so that some people were against Stevenson because he was against offshore drilling. Grandmother was trying to get all that logically worked out in her mind.

She also shared something else with us. "Papa is so mad," she said, "because those damn oil people won't keep his gate closed, and his cows got out. They keep promising they won't do that." Papa was then about ninety years old and had to get on his horse and pull his cattle back into the pasture. Fred asked, "What are they doing by coming on your land?" Papa jumped into the conversation and said, "Well, do you see those electric wires out there? A sleazy oil company came up and found oil next to Gack-u's [a Comanche name for grandmother] land and there are some Comanches making lots of money off the oil leases."

The oil companies didn't take care of their slush ponds or other things and they killed all the creeks and water supply within a ten-mile radius. In those days they had pumper families, white families, who lived out near the pumps and managed them. Pumper families were all over the countryside. My best girlfriend's father was a pumper. The oil companies didn't have a water supply because everywhere was so polluted that the only available water was on Grandmother's land from a spring that fed one of our little creeks. Well, Grandmother made a deal that if the oil company would furnish water to her house and yard and keep the fences up, keep the two gates closed where they had to drive the pump to maintain it, they could use her water.

She told us they weren't living up to the deal because they would cut her water off and not tell her, so she wondered if Fred could talk to them. "Let me see your contract," he said. She said she didn't have one, so Fred made some inquiries. First he asked the oil companies if they went

through the Bureau of Indian Affairs. No, they hadn't. Then Fred told them that we were going to sue their ass for trespassing and confiscate all their equipment until they did right. Well, they went to court and it was the most amazing result. Fred got Gack-u's back payments, dating from the beginning of their relationship. The oil companies had to pay for the utilities, the pipeline, everything because they were on her land and had not gone through the process via the Bureau of Indian Affairs. He made her tons of money off the water. While the rest were making money off the oil, she was making money off the water.

My grandparents believed Fred was a miracle man. They loved him anyway, but for him to be able to do that for them was wonderful. And all this happened because the oil company workers didn't close the gates.

There's more to the story. One day we were back in Walters and Fred ran into the son of a family friend. The boy said he was in school and also had a summer job. Fred said, "That's good. Everybody's going into oil, so you can get some actual experience in the oil fields." The boy answered, "All I have to do is keep this one Indian family in water." Well, we just cracked up. My folks were always so proud of Fred. They referred to him as "our son-in-law." All the Comanches called him that.

PRACTICING LAW

Fred graduated from law school at the top of his class, but before that, while he was still a student, he interned for a big law firm in Oklahoma City. He spent most of his time lost in the library doing research for somebody else to present a case. Working for someone else wasn't what he wanted to do for the rest of his life. So he and one of our close friends decided that after graduation they were going to start their own law firm in Lawton, where Mother lived. Well, Fred's law partner got drafted. Fred had also signed up, but since he was married and had a child, he was exempt, even though he had been in ROTC. The other fellow was single and in the National Guard, so he went to Korea. That broke up our plans, but gave us a good opportunity.

Our banker in Lawton, J. C. Kennedy, took an interest in us, talked to some of his lawyer friends and told them about the circumstances. They

were interested in Fred, so he delivered his resume and was interviewed. All during this time, our plans were to drive to New Mexico to see my sister. We did that; we went through Palo Duro Canyon and up to Adobe Walls near Borger, Texas, where Fred had relatives. In fact, they were our neighbors when we were in school and had helped us many times by feeding us. While we were driving back to Borger from Adobe Walls, the sheriff found us and told us that we had an important long distance call. The law firm members had had their meeting and decided they wanted Fred to join the firm. That made a wonderful holiday for us.

Back in Lawton, after university life and a liberal environment and all types of political friends, we joined the Junior Chamber of Commerce and the Comanche County Historical Society. By doing so, we lowered the average age of members to sixty-five years. We were about twenty at the time and everybody else was around seventy. Fred's law offices were in J. C. Kennedy's bank in downtown Lawton. He and the head of the law firm became Fred's mentors. The law firm was the largest in Lawton at the time and very prestigious.

A NEW COMANCHE PATH

When Fred first started practicing law, we were going to Comanche churches, and Fred was learning how to sing our songs and speak our language. We would take my grandmother out to a church in Deyo. She helped start that Deyo Mission.[1] The name comes from the first minister there who was one of the few that the Comanches liked. The rest of the churches had descriptive names like the yellow church, the brown church. I translated the sermons so Fred could catch on and start to understand the language. After church on Sundays we had lunch and walked all over the Wichita Mountains. Fred was very much into history and had read accounts of the Europeans who came through that area, or military expeditions. We tried to follow as close as possible the information in the books, such as the kinds of grass and kinds of animals that were here at the time. We described all the plants the Comanches ate, with the help of my grandmother, who talked about

them as Fred wrote down her description. We often had a picnic, built a little fire, and cooked potatoes and steak out there. Sometimes we ran into a nest of rattlesnakes. With that exception those are very pleasant memories, particularly taking Grandmother with us and asking her questions.

For years and years the Comanches had been members of what was called the KCA, an entity created by the BIA that included the Kiowa, Comanche, and Apache tribes in Oklahoma. Unbelievable. The government didn't respect the differences among us. To them, we were all just Indians. The Kiowas had the swing vote and the Comanches were out of the loop, so we wanted to have our own tribal government. The Kiowas had borrowed money in the 1960s to buy farm equipment and weren't paying the money back, so all three tribes had to pay their debt. There were about four of five things happening at once that the Comanches didn't approve of, and they wanted to break away from the KCA but didn't know how to do it.

Fred looked into it and found the Oklahoma Intercourse Act. What a name for a legislative act (it means they screwed us). All the tribes were organized under that particular legislation in Oklahoma but it contained nothing that said the Comanches couldn't break away. Fred did the research, drew up the papers, and got the boiler plate constitution that everybody has. That was written in the 1930s, actually during the Roosevelt era because the Roosevelt administration was concerned about what to do with the Indians during the recovery period after the Depression. At that time one of Mabel Dodge Lujan's salon attendants was the top man in the BIA, a man named John Collier, who believed the United States government needed to recognize Indian governments and work through those governments.[2] Good for him, but he never recommended that Indians should have a convention or what should go into their constitutions. Consequently, we all have the same form of government that doesn't fit the tribes, socially or culturally. We are still confronted with those problems today.

Fred wrote up the papers for the tribe to go on its own and petitioned the government. We had so many Indian supporters, partially because

Fred was out there among them all the time, learning the Comanche language. They loved it because they could speak to him in our language. People from the tribe came to our house when it was convenient for Fred and they spent all hours of the night together. Fred loved it because they got into telling stories. I remember that John Crow, one of the big guys in the BIA, asked why we wanted to be independent and claimed that we wouldn't even be in existence after a while anyway. We had a big vote and it literally tore up our families, particularly the Kiowa relatives with whom we had intermarried. We had "yes" and "no" families. We were a "yes" family. In my family, my great-aunt first went with the "yes" Comanches. My great-uncle said "no," so she became a "no." And then I had a Kiowa aunt who was a "yes" person. It was so emotional. God, how deeply it hurt.

The split from KCA was a major event for the Comanche tribe. Tribal members who favored the split were called the "yes" people. They believed that remaining part of the KCA would enable the Kiowas and the Kiowa-Apaches to obtain a disproportionate share of the land claim money. Comanches not in favor of the disaffiliation were called the "no" people. They argued that three tribes were politically stronger than one could be. The "yes" faction succeeded because, according to anthropologist Morris Foster, "its leaders used a typical short-term economic argument that played on community solidarity instead of longer term issues of Comanche-Anglo relations." The other half of the equation—the reason why the "no" faction failed, was "because its major constituency, those Comanches who subsisted almost entirely from lease and per capita payments, had declined in number since the war."[3] This vote signaled a major change in the philosophy of the tribe as well. With the success of the "yes" vote, it became clear that a younger generation of Comanches was challenging the older leadership and bringing the possibility of a new structure to the attention of tribal members.

Ever since we came to recognize this as one of the issues in Indian country, it has become so frustrating for tribes and the government to make programs work for Indians. They say, "We'll invite you to the White House. We'll have an Indian desk and treat you like other

minorities, but we have not incorporated you yet into the central system."
We have always been outside, no matter how hard we try.

FREDDIE AND THE INDIAN

In Lawton, when Fred was just starting his law practice, I learned to
play bridge but hated it. I played with the white ladies who were so
engrossed with the game. I didn't play that well, so I was embarrassed
and said many times that I wouldn't do it again. But, of course, I did, at
least for a short time. Fred took up golf and was gone quite a bit, playing
with the other lawyers out at our funny little golf course near the airport.
He had represented the golf course in a small lawsuit and they gave him
a set of clubs as a thank-you. He also joined the Rotary Club, which was
respected in Lawton. We had fun in the Junior Chamber of Commerce
because they were all our peers, dentists and doctors. We didn't think
we would be the middle-class establishment, but I guess we were. Our
banker and Ned Shepler, the editor of the *Lawton Constitution*, became
our friends. It was the story of our lives: older people always liked us.
We liked being around them, and they loved us. We were the youngest
set of people in that group, the hierarchy of the town.

As I made friends along the way, I learned that most of the young
women from the upper economic group belonged to the Junior League.
People told me I should join. I agreed and gave it a try. Well, they turned
me down. I was dumbfounded. Later, when Fred was elected to the state
senate, they wanted me to join but I didn't. When I first applied, he was
just a young lawyer in town married to an Indian, and they had never
had an Indian among their membership. Instead, I joined the Lawton
Women's Forum, a group that had Mrs. Shepler and Mrs. Kennedy as
members. A very wealthy woman had left some money to the city and
they built a nice meeting place for the community to use. The Lawton
Women's Forum managed it for the estate. They made me an officer
early on; they were pleased to have me, and it felt just right. Again, I
functioned better around older people than with my own peers. This
was a civic women's group, comprised of mostly college women who
weren't working. They would have been in the women's movement, had

it come along then. They tried to enlighten themselves and make a better community by helping to build parks and supporting worthy causes. I thoroughly enjoyed it and quit the bridge club right away.

I became pregnant while we were living in Lawton, and carried the baby to term, but there were complications. The cord was around the baby's neck and she died during birth. I believe Fred suffered more than I did over our loss. I couldn't stand to look at him; it was just devastating. Fred was with me when I was giving birth at home, but there wasn't anything we could have done differently at the hospital anyway. No one realized the cord was around her neck. We had picked out the name of Elizabeth Carl, after my sister Billie's name. We had a lot of fun preparing Kathryn for the baby. With Dr. Spock in one hand and Kathryn in the other, we'd read up on how to prepare a child. I felt bad for Kathryn because she was built up to the wonderful fact that she was going to have a sister or a brother. Fred and Grandmother more or less took over and dealt with the whole situation because I couldn't. The baby is buried out at Deyo, Oklahoma, at the church. I didn't go to the funeral. I was too depressed and it took me a while to get over that. But then we gradually got back into action again and into community activities.

We were just settling in to Lawton in the late 1950s or early 1960s when an Oklahoma state senator, Bill Logan, died of cancer and left a vacancy in office. The fellow who was our representative at the time was also a lawyer and had been in Lawton for years, but wasn't very visionary. He and Fred were interested in running for the vacant seat. Fred worked to get the support of J. C. Kennedy and Ned Shepler. They agreed and helped him get some funds together. It was important support from his law firm. Well, here we were in the race. I wasn't very involved in the day-to-day campaigning because I was making a living for us.

From the first day, we sat beside each other, though, planning every minute. We started off with my Comanche relatives. I notified everybody. Along with that we addressed post cards to every organization, announcing that we were running for office and needed help, financially

or as a volunteer. It is so important to ask people to help. Everyone wants to be asked. If you do that they can't say later, "Well, he never asked me to vote for him." Fred ran in Comanche County and Cotton County, our new county and our home county.

Fred's folks still lived at Porter Hill and his sister lived nearby, in Elgin. Both towns were in the political district. Whenever he campaigned in Walters he next went to Elgin to establish some identity. He said, "I'm Fred Harris and I'm running for the senate. I sure would like your support. You might know my sister Sue. She married J. T. Stauffer." He met several men in a country store and as he shook hands with them and gave them his little speech, one of the men said, "I'm John Stauffer." Oops. We had just met him once at the wedding. How embarrassing.

Back home in Walters we had friends, relatives, and classmates, so we put up a good campaign. Our opponent had been established there for five years, but our Comanche relatives got out and campaigned for us. My great-uncle Bill, out at Cache, even got into it. When I needed a baby-sitter, his wife stayed with Kathryn. Mother was right around the corner and we usually took her with us. Well, to make a long story short, Fred won and he was one of the youngest members ever of the Oklahoma state senate.

We blossomed out then. The legislature was in session from Monday through Thursday, every two years. I went to the state senate every other week from Lawton. Those were really my glory years—jumping into a campaign, getting elected, and then jumping right into the state legislature and getting to know all those people. We were both very young, about twenty-five years old. In order for me to go to Oklahoma City to be with him, we again had to have a baby-sitter for Kathryn. At first I called on my great-aunt. She was so terrific and her kids were grown. My uncle helped her. At night a young black woman from Lawton baby-sat. Her father was an educator with the school system and that's what she was working toward also. During the times she couldn't make it, she called upon a friend of hers, Mary Jackmon, who became a lifelong friend.

In Oklahoma City we got invited to all the big to-do things. Immediately we swung into the center of town and knew what was going on everywhere. Fred was already a Mason; it's one of those old secret male things. He became a Shriner too because it was politically correct to do. I teased him and made fun of all this. He teased me back about the secret society and said he couldn't tell me anything about it because it was so secret. He said, "I sure would like to share with you but. . . ." Drove me nuts.

After Fred was elected, I became pregnant with Byron. Big as a mountain, I'd go to the state senate. A senator could allow someone to sit on the floor with him, so I sat by his desk on the floor of the senate. One of the things that we did was use each other in the best sense of the word. He was verbal and I was still the stoic Indian, calling on all the things that helped me get through school and protect myself. Because I had always avoided anything that might be hurtful, I used all my senses in knowing how to read people's body language. Fred depended on my interpretation of behavior and especially liked me to go to any of his committee hearings and react to them. He was in one position to hear something and I, as part of the audience, was in another position.

This was the relationship we built up through the years. He relied on my evaluation of people and always wanted to know what I thought and what my observation was. I was less critical than he was. I always looked for the best in people and told him that. I could also see how people cared for each other, a little or a great deal. I interpreted relationships for him.

In my stoic Indian period, back when I was younger and couldn't or wouldn't express myself very well, I pulled my hair back very severely to look older and dressed in very conservative clothes. We were such kids ourselves and were just thrown into this political situation, but our partnership was one of the best things in our relationship. I depended on him to be our voice. He was so articulate. Because I didn't speak, my senses were much more attuned to what was going on. When you have the ability to speak, you lose some of those senses.

No other senate wives came to Oklahoma City in those days and women senators were unheard of at the time. No candidate had even included his wife in campaigning back then. Nobody but Fred. In fact, I got lectured a couple of times out on the campaign trail because I was campaigning for him. I was told that a wife's place was in the home. It was well before women's involvement in politics. Imagine, women told me they didn't believe in women in politics, and the men I met would kind of cower. I paid particular attention to women, shaking their hands and asking for their vote for Fred. It was a shock to me to learn that the attitude was so strong against active women. And it must have been a shock to them to learn later that Fred had been elected!

One of our favorite senators lived in western Oklahoma. We visited him at a hearing there and had dinner with him and his wife. At that time they were quite elderly. He said to his wife, "I wish you had gone with me and been part of the senate." She answered, "You know, I always wished you had asked me." See, all those years they had never communicated with each other. Not me. The Oklahoma senate pro tem, Don Baldwin (whom we named Byron after because Don meant so much to us), took Fred under his wing.[4] Because Fred was so hardworking, doing all the drudge work, all the things that needed to be done, he proved himself valuable in the senate and they recognized his hard work. Don Baldwin took up Fred and asked him to move in. They had bedrooms and a common living room in an Oklahoma City hotel while the session was on. Actually it was a suite. At the time, in the 1960s, Oklahoma was dry and we had to buy liquor from a bootlegger, but that was easy enough. Everybody came to see Baldwin, as president of the senate, so I acted as hostess and poured drinks and served them. Boy, those guys could drink. And smoke! You couldn't see across the room because of the smoke — the old smoke-filled room.

One of the best parts of the entire experience was that the older guys again paid attention to us and made us feel important. Fred and I were occasionally invited out to dinner with them. This bothered the younger senators, who said, "God damn, don't bring your wife to restaurants." You see, they were out with their secretaries having dinner. Wives just

didn't come to Oklahoma City, but we were a new breed of folks. It was just absolutely fabulous. There were a bunch of characters around. For example, one big old guy dressed in western clothes and looked like a cornstalk. He would talk about his aunt Millie when he introduced legislation and always spoke about how his relatives would do with a particular piece of legislation. He had an eastern Oklahoma accent and gave us a nickname, Freddie and the Indian. Not offensive. Other older legislators called me Comanche. It was a form of acceptance.

At one point during his term Fred was head of the mental health committee. It was a time when we were going through those horrible snake-pit days. He asked me and one of his staff members to visit a mental institution because if he went, he would see it from his perspective, and he wanted information from our point of view. We went, and didn't give the institution much notice. These are just forgotten people. The staff member took notes. Then we gave a report to Fred, and he was able to enact a great deal of legislation to improve mental health conditions. We had visited six state-controlled and segregated mental hospitals. I think that was every last one in Oklahoma. Once you visit places like that, you will always be committed to improve mental health conditions. After that, I spent several years working in the area of mental health, but reporting to Fred on those conditions was probably the most outstanding thing I did in those days.

As I was the wife of a state senator, people came to see me about many things. One was a young couple who asked that I meet with them and representatives from the black community about integration. Well, we had never thought about what blacks had to go through, and I was interested. We met with a woman who ran the segregated USO and a social worker, Betty Owens, whose husband, Eugene, was a doctor. At first we sat and talked in Lawton and then agreed to meet again and bring food for the next session. We began to involve other people and it grew like magic. We would have a covered-dish supper and then talk about the issues and integrating Lawton, particularly the restaurants. What kinds of things should we be doing? How can we affect change? The woman who owned a greasy spoon downtown, where most of the military from

Fort Sill ate, said, "Well, if we don't want to eat with Negroes, why do they want to eat with us?" That was her level of rationale. As a member of the mayor's committee on integration, Fred worked along with us and tried to force the city fathers to make policy. We formed what we called the Honcho Group during the days of the late 1960s activism. Everybody had to chair it so there wouldn't be any fighting for leadership. Being a leader of an integration movement wasn't very popular, so we agreed that everyone had to hold that position. We gave assignments. If someone was familiar with a particular restaurant, he was appointed to integrate it by talking to the owners. My God, it worked. We used social pressure from peer groups. We went quietly to them without fanfare and asked them respectfully to integrate their establishments. About ten complied. There were always one or two holdouts.

The hard part was formulating the strategy. We formed committees and fought among ourselves. The Catholic Church became involved through one of our neighbors. Later on, when we showed some success, we had an unofficial representative from Fort Sill join us. Fort Sill was integrated at the time, and through our neighbor's (the same one who involved the Catholic Church) influence with the commanding officer, some black officers became involved, just to socialize. They finally had someplace to go. We used our influence with the military to integrate certain restaurants, telling the owners, "We understand that there's a movement to integrate at Fort Sill, and if you don't, they'll put your restaurant off limits." We were so smart. We just sat down and thought of it in human relations terms. It was a real study. No one in our group had ever done anything like this before. We resorted to the threat of economic blackmail and damn if we didn't integrate most every restaurant in Lawton. With the cooperation of the military, though, we finally had to call one greasy spoon off limits because the owner simply would not integrate. It had been a favorite place for the soldiers to go late in the evening, and losing business almost broke her. She finally gave in.

Next, the Honcho Group opened up housing and jobs. And then there was the only public swimming pool. They didn't allow blacks to swim there, so we put every pressure in the book on them, even got

the mayor involved. By that time we were a group of about thirty-five people, including blacks. It was the first time we had ever had a chance to socialize with blacks and get to know them as human beings. Our group picketed the swimming pool and actually closed it down. The army put it off limits. The fact that we were successful here, too, gave us so much more credibility.

We served wine and beer at our Honcho meetings, and when the business of the day was done, we just sat around and drank. Fred said, "You all are having too much fun."

One night my sister and her husband were staying with us, and I invited them to go to our meeting. Sister said, "Oh, no. I'm not going and I'm not going to take Ray." Ray just loved to get under my skin. Sister said, "I know that Ray will make a mistake," but I thought he knew how to behave better than that. Ray said, "Sure enough. I want to go and I'll behave." After dinner at our meeting place, we sat around the living room having a drink and discussing politics. Ray said, "I knew a fellow like that. Damn nigger." Sister almost cried, could have died right there on the spot, but our hostess was gracious and let him off the hook.

ADVOCATING INDIAN ISSUES

About this time the University of Oklahoma asked Fred to come to a weeklong symposium at the Southwest Center for Human Relations Studies. They planned to study black-white relations and labor-management relations. He couldn't make it, so he suggested they invite me and added that they would then get my contribution, I'd share it with him, and they would have his support. Two for one. So, I spent a week in Norman as one of two Indians involved in the group. The other was a man who was head of the Concho Indian School. The talk was about black-white relationships and about discrimination. Nothing about Indians.

So, I asked, "Well, what about Indians?" Our learned professors from the University of Oklahoma and other learned people from around the state thought the Bureau of Indian Affairs took care of Indian issues. When they said that, I just went crazy. I became a blabbering idiot

because I had such a hard time expressing myself. They couldn't see that they were part of the problem, and they were not solving Indian problems. I finally burst into tears because I couldn't articulate how I felt, and I so wanted them to understand. I embarrassed the shit out of them with my tears. The other Indian was what we call an "apple" [red on the outside, white on the inside], thoroughly indoctrinated, and here I was, this funny little young Indian woman who couldn't say two words. We became good friends, and he helped me start Oklahomans for Indian Opportunity, but I'm getting ahead of myself.

As part of the center's program we organized two ventures. A member who was in law enforcement and had done human relations work in St. Louis went to his counterparts and social workers in Oklahoma City and interviewed them. Still in the late 1960s, the University of Oklahoma professors and I decided to interview the Anadarko Bureau of Indian Affairs people about Indian issues. We made three appointments with three different people (all of these people had Ph.D.s and other degrees) and set specific times, but they didn't cooperate. Finally, one person appeared and I said, "How would you like to be my grandmother who doesn't speak English all that well? She would come here to try to find information affecting her, her property, or her income, and nobody appears." That's what the Indian people run into. There's no communication and they treat their clients like shit. I learned to use that word to make a point.

The Bureau of Indian Affairs is not an agency that is really an advocate for Indians. It's a controlling institution that keeps people from doing what they could do. The other Indian in the group, the guy who was teaching at Concho Indian School, didn't say anything. A bureaucrat. I complained about those Indian schools, too. Concho had the highest suicide rate of all. The suicide and dropout rates were pathetic all over Indian country and there was no literature for us to look at that explained why we Indians had such high rates. Nothing addressed the problems that Indian children faced.

When the police officer returned from Oklahoma City, he reported that he had been told there were no problems with Indian schools because

"they take care of their own and they had an underground where they smoked peyote and drugs, and had dens similar to opium dens where they used peyote." Imagine that. All kinds of stupid fantasies. The police officer came back so overwhelmed by the problems that he said, "Boy, we need to know more." Other social workers said that the urban Indians were a real mess, that they couldn't do anything for themselves and they [the social workers] had to do everything for them. The university professors asked what they could do. "Come and visit some of my folks," I answered. They agreed. At that time an older, gentle, and beautiful man who was part of our group and kept inspiring me said, "You go to the top of the mountain and you see all these good things. You're just dragging the rest of us along." I was so grateful for those words. Well, we continued on with our work and were joined by a group of Comanches, mostly my relatives, who responded to an open invitation I issued. Many of those who participated in our group were members of the Comanche Tribal Council. We called what we were doing "Indian education." Word spread, and so many people, Indian and non-Indian, joined us that we moved to the Fort Sill Indian School and rented a room out there for our meetings. We invited non-Indian experts to talk with us, once we determined what we needed to learn. We were educating ourselves and at the same time talking about embarrassing moments. For example, if I went with Fred to a hotel or big restaurant, I didn't know the proper etiquette. I felt so self-conscious and thought everybody was looking at me. One of the best things that happened was that the older Comanches also talked about embarrassing things that happened to them as they were growing up. Comanches do that real well. It took some of the pressure off the rest of us Indians there because it made us feel less pitiful. I remember one of our tribal council members saying that he had been on the council only a few months when he went to a big restaurant to eat. He carried his briefcase and pretended to be a big boss man. He sat down and watched everybody to see how to act. Other people were making a big deal about the napkins, and his kept slipping off his lap, so he tucked it in his pants. During the meal he made his points and really felt good about himself. He got up, paid his check, and

was outside before he realized he still had his napkin tucked in his pants. People told funny stories about themselves, just like that one. It helped the mood and attitude of the group.

One time—can't remember exactly when—we had a reception at my house and invited the mayor and other Lawton officials who were interested in human relations. We Indians had to learn a level of comfort with the white people, had to go up to them and talk, had to meet the officials. It was very hard. There were Indians among us who were friends of those white people, but to come into a room and just start talking with the mayor and other city dignitaries was so difficult. Still, we couldn't stand off and not participate.

OKLAHOMANS FOR INDIAN OPPORTUNITY

Out of that nucleus we started Oklahomans for Indian Opportunity (oio).[5] The association began in my living room. We became the first statewide Indian organization, got a great board put together, but couldn't be funded directly because we weren't a reservation group. So, we had to use our university contacts and get the University of Utah to fund our program in Oklahoma.

Our first oio project in the late 1960s was to determine why there was such a large school dropout rate among Indian children. For example, we learned that in Ponca City, Oklahoma, the population of Indian kids in the first grade was 75 percent. By the time they got to the sixth or seventh grade, it fell to about 2 percent. With just a little research it became very, very clear that Indian children were dropping out at enormous rates. We felt we wanted to stop it somehow and keep them in school. So at first we interviewed juniors and seniors in high school, but they had built up a protective veneer so the process of getting an education wouldn't hurt them. They couldn't tell us what was painful about school, so we went to the lower grades. There, the children said they felt humiliated almost every day by teachers calling them "squaws" and using all those other old horrible terms. Most of them had such a low self-esteem anyway that they felt they couldn't achieve, that Indians just couldn't make it. Some Indian kids got good marks in the lower grades, but when they got to

the age of consciousness or puberty, they got turned off and dropped out, usually from the seventh, eighth, or ninth grades.

These kids felt something was wrong with them, that the system, the whole colonial madness, said anybody in authority knew better then they did. They never questioned it. They learned that the Indian culture had no value, and that because they were part of that culture, they had no value. In order to have any value, they had to become like white people.

To be able to achieve, or go to college, Indian people had to have protection from pain. My stoic period was my protection from getting hurt. I was absolutely silent and showed no reaction to what was being said, so no one knew if they were hurting me or not. It directed attention away from abusing me. The Indian people who had made it to college had built whatever protection they needed to overcome the pain, even though the system had hurt them.

In the process of building self-esteem, the students told us what the teachers said to them. It was so dehumanizing that we in OIO proposed reverse role-playing to demonstrate to the authorities what was going on. They agreed, so the students then became the teachers and the teachers were the students. It was so humiliating to the teachers that many of them cried and we had to stop. I don't know if they realized what they had been doing and that's why they were crying, or they were crying because they were so embarrassed. Some of them got angry. We literally had to stop one performance because people became so agitated. Others were so sorry about their behavior.[6]

OIO working on these kids' self-esteem really bothered some locals. We got thrown out of Watonga, Oklahoma, for example, and one of the university professors with us was accused of being a communist. In eastern Oklahoma around the Ponca City area, the BIA fought us and said they would report that we had gotten an Office of Economic Opportunity grant.[7] Said they would inform members of Congress on us, and they did, but we had received only flow-through funds, which was legitimate. The BIA officials told Congress, "These are our Indians," and they didn't want people from western Oklahoma coming in and messing with people from the Muskogee area.

But we organized them with the support of the Comanches. We did little things like show them how to use commodities and give them recipes. Talk about poor, pitiful people. The trading stores owned them. They used to sign over their checks. They never had cash money, ever, because they always owed and could never get out of debt. Also, they didn't have water wells. They had shallow ponds where they got their water, much of it dirty. Later, when Fred was in the United States Senate, we brought the Office of Economic Opportunity (OEO) and Environmental Protection Agency (EPA) people to eastern Oklahoma and gave them a bus tour. They saw the people had their toilets up on a hill and body wastes leached through to the water. It was terrible. Most of the folks were on welfare and received commodities, which the kids refused to eat because they were of such poor quality. OIO tried to create good things for the people, such as helping them develop a hog farm and holding summer camps for the kids in which they were taught judo and self-discipline, among other things. The BIA authorities thought we were teaching them to have an uprising. You wouldn't believe the kinds of things we heard.

Finally, out of total frustration, I went around the BIA to continue to help the eastern Oklahomans. I applied what I had learned previously, which is if anyone becomes a block, if anyone stops you from what you are trying to accomplish, figure out a way around them. If you can't convince them in an intellectual discussion or an emotional appeal (I have used everything, even seduction to a certain point) and if they are still immovable, just figure out a way to go around them. There's always somebody over the immovable person, and you can approach that person as well. Even if you have to dig a hole under them or build a bridge over them. Just figure it out. Try everything first before you absolutely give up. [If you are successful] the immovable person will then say, "Well, this is wonderful," and will give you a lot of credit.

OIO also challenged the kids by donating books about tribes—bought with OEO funds—to school libraries. (There were a few small foundation grants, but they didn't come until later. In the early days we had to front the money all the way through.) We said we wanted everybody, Indians

and non-Indians, to read them. We spoke to students who were non-Indians and asked them to question their Indian friends as to what they heard and read. Then we told the Indian students to get caught up on the history of their own tribes because their classmates would be asking.

In some schools we made speeches and met with officials like the football coach or the principal. School administrations showed us that they loved their Indians by forcing a poor Choctaw football player, for example, to wear a Comanche headdress for me and stand up on the stage. I always made the point that I knew the kids were embarrassed when they had to wear a headdress that was inappropriate for their tribe.

Was it discrimination? I find that most discrimination is ignorance. What is so painful is that those who discriminate often don't realize they are doing it. It isn't direct, like in the Deep South when the dogs were set upon the blacks. When it's indirect, it causes much more pain because you can't fight it, and nobody articulates it. That's how I felt while I was growing up. I found ways of dealing with it, but most Indians felt something was wrong with them. The whole of the dominant society was telling us how to behave, and that wasn't natural for me and was uncomfortable. I could feel that conflict between the cultural values. Even though our kids were trying their best, when they discovered they couldn't handle it, they dropped out of school. Or they found enough protection to go on. Or they incorporated enough of the dominant society's values that they became acceptable to some faction of the institution. The whole idea of self-esteem is involved. How do you teach it? How do you grow with it?

For me and my generation, if your grandparents didn't raise you, you became a victim. If your parents raised you, it was almost like a different world. I don't know how people survived it. To me, that's the miracle of the decade.

Some people adopted the totally new way. In my family we became educated because we could. We had the Allotment Act and we didn't have that bonding of reservation life, like other tribes did. It makes a difference. There are a whole bunch of Indian people like my mother

who became planners in government institutions, Indian Health Service, or the BIA. Officially, Indian women could only become lower caregivers, like nurses' aides. Mother never became a true nutritionist although she did all the planning; the other person had the title. Indian women could also become teachers. Men could only become preachers or farmers.

Most people lived on their lease money [also known as grass money]. There are all kinds of stories about lease money.[8] Some of the saddest had to do with people asking, "Can you loan me money until my lease money comes in?" Almost all of the historical Comanches were free spirits and the government couldn't understand that. Officials brought sheep to the Comanches because sheep herding suited the Navajos so well! Well, what did the Comanches do? They shot them in target practice with a bow and arrow. No Comanches could eat them. On Papa's farm, we had cattle. When we needed a little money, he sold off a calf.

About the time OIO got under way in the late 1960s, the Choctaw tribe had mistakenly signed an agreement to be terminated.[9] They started fighting it when they realized what would happen to them, thanks to a bunch of us who helped bring the ills of termination into the light.[10] Fortunately, the history of what had happened to the Menominee tribe had come out, and their stories were similar.[11] The government tried to convince the Choctaws that they would be better off if they ended their relationship with the government. [Being independent] would allow them to be on their own and to do what they always wanted, so the government said. Well, we spread the word around and brought Ada Deer into the picture and she talked to them, told the ills of the Menominee termination to the Choctaws and to the tribes of Oklahoma.[12] The Choctaws then rejected termination and were able to stop it. That was thrilling, and OIO had been involved!

OIO worked hard at addressing important matters. We used Comanche ways to make all our efforts work, ordinarily through group decisions. We didn't have a power struggle to see who would be the chairman of the group. One person would be the speaker, but everybody would be a leader. In that way, nobody could take it over, but everybody had responsibility in making our effort work. Our focus was community

action. There was no guidance available at the time, so we just plowed our own field. Everything we did broke new ground.

It has been so rewarding to me to know that I have made a difference through 010. When I'm at a low ebb, or having a difficult time, someone or something has always come along to help me over it. Some helpers have even been white people who have given me that little extra boost that has allowed me to continue. I would like to be that kind of person for somebody else.

IN THE CAPITAL

5

There are points in my life when the pain comes back . . . makes me feel like

I have to throw up.

In the 1950s and early 1960s many women took second place to their husbands, brothers, or sons. Only a few ventured forward to claim their own spotlight. LaDonna was becoming one of them, step by step. Though it occasionally sounds like she identified herself through Fred, LaDonna grew to see herself as much more than Fred's wife. She was an individual, a full partner with her husband, and someone he needed in order to reach *their* goals. And, as husband Fred was becoming prominent, LaDonna was moving toward her own celebrity. One major landmark along the way was their life together in Washington.

~

While Fred was in the last year of his term as an Oklahoma state senator [1958], he decided to run for governor. I wasn't very involved in that campaign and isn't it interesting that it doesn't stand out in my mind? We lost to J. Howard Edmonson, a very flamboyant, Robert Redford type, small and slight.[1] Somehow you didn't get the idea he was short, because he had a big stock of reddish-blond hair. Despite our loss, the campaign allowed Fred to gain statewide visibility and name recognition.

He had already earned a good reputation in the state senate for being a hard worker, and taking on those jobs that nobody really liked to do. He also learned all the floor skills and how to use the rules of the floor to get things done.

When U.S. Senator Robert S. Kerr died in office in the early 1960s, Edmonson resigned the governor's chair and was then appointed by his replacement to Kerr's seat.[2] After that term expired, there was a special election, and we beat him easily. Then, however, we had to run against Bud Wilkinson, the great white hope of Oklahoma, who "brought pride" back to the Okies and the Okie mentality through football. The ou football team was the pride of Oklahoma.

During that 1963–64 campaign, Fred sent me places without him but with other staff people and campaign people. We went to communities like Muskogee, where the Edmonsons lived, and Guthrie, and Stillwater. Those towns were ultraconservative, and he had pretty well written them off, deciding there wasn't any sense in spending his time and money there, but I went anyway. I was uncomfortable in Guthrie because of being an Indian, and in Stillwater I felt not angry so much as hurt because of the discrimination I sensed—a flashback from high school days.

There are points in my life when the pain comes back, like posttraumatic stress syndrome. Makes me feel like I have to throw up, like food turns sour. These are the things I worked all my life to rid other people of so they wouldn't hurt. The hurt way deep inside is so demeaning, and, unfortunately, people really don't know any better. In Stillwater, people talked down to me, patronized me. They were so ignorant. It feels just like gall rising up and choking me, making me want to cry. If something is directed at me, it gets to this inner pain and then I get angry and go into my crazy Comanche woman role. In any case, in Stillwater I collected the people who were working for us and reinforced their commitment to Fred's election. That was one of my major roles in the entire campaign. Then we organized our hometown, Lawton. Somebody got us the state fair barn for rent, and we made our own fence straddlers, those posters over the barbed-wire fences. An architect

designed them, and we hand silk-screened them. It was great fun. To this day I don't know how we won. Must have been because of our hands-on approach, though. We also had coffee klatches [small groups brought together for a purpose, sometimes political] and went into the black communities because we had great contacts there. Oklahoma had a large black population, particularly in Tulsa and the southeastern part of the state. We really were a big hit in those communities. The fact that I went with Fred to these locations and also into homes made a big impression. It showed our sincerity regarding our liberal attitude about race. Another thing: the black fraternities and sororities were a big help. Word had gotten around that we were friends of black people. In later years they honored me, which was very rewarding.

Our black friends in Muskogee during this same 1963–64 campaign were our nucleus of support there and they wanted somebody from the campaign to come over and talk with them. They said if Fred couldn't go, I was the next best thing. One of my memories of going to campaign in Muskogee was that a rumor had gotten out saying Kerr money was backing us. It made us look good. We didn't have Kerr money but we were eking out just enough funds to keep the campaign going.

This time Fred's mother got involved and did some campaigning for us. She was effective among the elderly ladies. Grandmother went with us too. We had Harris Headliner dresses, and Gack-u wore a Harris Headliner shawl. What's a Harris Headliner? Our volunteers needed a name and somebody came up with the brilliant idea of having broadcloth dresses with headlines in the material about Fred, such as Harris says this and Harris does that. Our funds were so limited that our volunteers had to buy their own material and make their own dresses.

Since almost everybody in Oklahoma claims to be part Indian, our campaign literature identified me as "LaDonna Harris, enrolled Comanche." Our public relations people asked if they could leave out that information because they needed the space for a message. Fred said, "No. It might not mean anything to you, but we will work to try to get out the Indian vote. These words, 'enrolled member,' mean LaDonna is a real Indian." Gack-u loved going with us. She was so excited and

we introduced her to everyone. On the train trip we made from the western side of the state, we picked up Democrats who were running for local offices. We had a Harris campaign song that the volunteers, our kids, and Gack-u would sing along the way. Laura was about three or four years old then, having been born in 1961 when we were running for governor. It had been an easy pregnancy, a breeze. I had delivered in the hospital but didn't like it. I preferred delivering at home, being in the middle of the room with all the attention.

During our race for the U.S. Senate in 1963, the other senator from Oklahoma, Mike Moroney, supported us.[3] He was an Adlai Stevenson person, a supporter of Eleanor Roosevelt, both people I like to think of. Through Mike we met President Lyndon Johnson, who was running for reelection in 1963–64. Johnson was a towering big guy whose hands just swallowed you, and he had a manner of invading your space. He'd put his arm around you and get right into your face and say, "Goddammit, we just gotta do this." If you were in favor, he'd shake hands real hard and pat you on the back in that kind of preacher, domineering southern way.

The Vietnam War was on but the country hadn't yet turned on the war so severely. Johnson was nice to us, and we had planned to ask his help in running against Bud Wilkinson, the great figure. But President Johnson took the opportunity to get after Mike Monroney, rather than listen to Mike pushing us. As soon as we walked in his office, Johnson said, "Goddammit Mike, what do you mean you can't help me on the Goddamn aviation?" We were so taken aback. Monroney was head of the Aviation Subcommittee, and I had no idea what this was all about, but Johnson knew Mike was sensitive and would never curse like that. Monroney cringed.

Finally, Johnson turned around and said, "Well, Fred, I could use some good old Oklahoma boys. I'm tired of all these Massachusetts people up here, all these people from the East Coast. We need some good old southern and southwest boys. You work hard down there and get elected." He didn't say much more because the polls, particularly the *Newsweek* poll, didn't show us favorably, indicating that Bud Wilkinson would win. Johnson was coming to Oklahoma to campaign, and we

tried to make arrangements beforehand to meet with him and get some pictures made. Remember, he was running against Barry Goldwater. Of course, he was also a sitting president, but he wouldn't set up a meeting, and that meant no pictures. But Fred's public relations guy got a television camera into a closed Democratic Party meeting, naturally including the president, to which Fred was invited. There was a chance of getting a shot of Fred with the president. Our PR guy somehow got the president cornered and stuck a microphone in his face. He said, "Mr. President, what do you think about Fred R. Harris?" The president said, "Well, if you send me old Fred, we'll nail the coonskin on the door and bring home the bacon." We blew it up as a television ad. That was our Lyndon Johnson endorsement. Oklahomans loved it. A lot of people know exactly what those words mean.

Fred wanted to campaign in every town in Oklahoma, so the first thing we did was divide up the state and decide how much time we would spend in each place, depending on the population centers. We have wild stories about all the things that happened, and there are one or two incidents in particular that I can't forget. During a visit to a certain town, Fred stopped off at the local newspaper. A reporter had written about our coming to town and had published a photo. The reporter said, "Yes, sir, Senator Harris, here's your picture." Well, it wasn't a picture of Fred at all, and he said so. The fellow said, "Oh, yes it is," and wouldn't accept no for an answer. Fred gave up and said, "Oh, I sure do thank you for the story."

We have story after story like that, including several related to air travel across Oklahoma. We'd land at night on runways that weren't lighted, so in advance we asked our supporters to drive to the landing strip and put their car lights on. It wasn't half so bad taking off as it was landing and some of those were made in pastures out in western Oklahoma. One time we landed in a pasture that was full of mounds that had been built to keep erosion from occurring. It nearly killed us to land there. Once we landed on the highway. We were coming in to the Will Rogers Airport in Tulsa, just over the river, and had a reporter with us who worked for the Tulsa newspaper. The plane's engine died.

The reporter told the pilot to head for the river; otherwise we'd hit the residences. The pilot said, "As soon as it hits, get out quick because it could catch fire." I was petrified. Just when our wheels touched the sand, the motor popped, and we got out. The reporter said, "Fred, do you know what Will Rogers's last words were to Wiley Post? They were 'Wiley Post, you son of a bitch'" and then added that she felt that way about the trip. Another time Fred and another fellow had an emergency situation where they had to land on a highway. They had dropped so low that they were about to hit one of the overpasses on a highway. For some reason the instruments didn't register how low they had gotten; it was below tree level. They had to set it down on the Turner Turnpike, which, fortunately, was wide enough. The first car that drove up was a highway patrol car with Governor Henry Bellmon in it. The local newspaper carried a story saying "Bellmon Comes to Senator's Rescue." Fred admitted it was a scary experience, but he kept flying, although with better pilots. Once I flew from Lawton to Hobart, where I was scheduled to speak at the high school. When the pilot talked, he lost altitude, and then he'd go back up, and then he'd go down again. We got lost and had to fly around a water tower to see where we were.

After a while I was so exhausted from campaigning and I could hear the kids back home saying they weren't getting along with whomever was baby-sitting, so I'd go home for about a week. I needed my kids. I got so hungry for them. Back on the campaign trail, Fred took one side of the street and I took the other and we'd meet our staffers at the end of the street. If we didn't have a friend in a particular town who had gone to law school with us and could set up a personal meeting, we had somebody hand out folders that announced Fred would be at a certain restaurant at a certain time. Everyone was invited to come and meet him and shake hands. Fred would say a few words and I'd go around, shake hands, ask for their support, and hand out literature. People need to be asked for their help, to be touched, so if Fred didn't ask them directly, I did. It helped. We also passed out postcards in barbershops and gave them to whittlers, the guys who sit outside on benches and don't have anything

to do but gossip. Fred took a lot of time with them and listened to their opinions.

Everybody is an opinion molder. You just have to have an opinion to be an opinion molder, and people will quote you. We told our volunteers to express their opinions and to say, "Well, I hear old Harris is really good and he's got a wonderful wife and he stands for this and that and is a good family man." We called our campaign workers opinion molders. We told them they were shaping other people's opinions by having one. It was such a simple concept, but studies indicate that is absolutely the way certain ideas get generated by someone choosing one person over another, someone saying, "I believe in this guy," and not being afraid to say it, not waiting until it's clear who's going to win and then stand up for that candidate. That philosophy helped us a great deal.

PARTNERSHIP

My grandmother was my grandfather's partner and I became that same type of partner to Fred, although in a different era. Indian women used to be stoic, but when I broke out of that I became a full partner to my husband, still reflecting Comanche values. In past campaigns people said there was "too much LaDonna," and it always came back to me second or thirdhand; but, very few said it out loud. Fred wouldn't have put up with it; it would have pissed him off. Even the one who carried the message would get chewed out if anybody criticized me for being in the campaign—because he wanted me there. It wasn't me pushing myself into this place. To criticize me would have been a personal criticism of him. He only mentioned something to me three times in a statewide campaign about someone saying there was too much of me. "Goddamn," he said. "Assholes. They don't understand the new politics, they don't understand this or that." Fred's defense of me always made me so proud, that I didn't give a darn what anybody thought. I am important. He always made me feel that way. I like to think that I did the same for him, that nobody would criticize him either.

Hubert Humphrey came to Oklahoma to campaign for us at sometime during those hectic months (I forget when), and he was really great.

He talked about our opponent, Bud Wilkinson, because both he and Wilkinson were from Minnesota. Humphrey said, "I'm proud of our Minnesotans, but I don't think you need one down here." I just loved him.

And then we won. What a thrill. We were on our way to Washington DC and Fred was a U.S. senator.

WASHINGTON DC

As soon as we got there in 1964, Hubert and Muriel Humphrey took us under their wing. He was vice president of the United States at the time. When I took tours of Oklahomans through the Capitol building, we would wind up in his office. He'd say, "Well, where's old Fred? Call him and tell him to come on over and have dinner. I have to make a speech, but after that we can eat and dance." The people from home were so impressed, especially when he posed with them for pictures. Hubert Humphrey was a people lover. He talked to you as if you were the most interesting person he had ever met. He paid attention and didn't look over your shoulder, as so many others did, to see if there was a more important individual around. I just loved him. He did so much for us in the United States Senate, something like what Don Baldwin did for Fred in the Oklahoma state senate.

The Robert Kennedys lived right around the corner from us in McLean, Virginia. Fred and Bobby Kennedy, Fritz Mondale, and another senator, Joe Tydings from Maryland, were four young and ambitious politicians, part of a new crop that were elected at the same time.[4] They called themselves the Knothole Gang and sat together in the back of the Senate. The Kennedys had a swimming pool and they invited the kids to come over and swim. We'd all go. It took a little while for me to get acquainted with Ethel Kennedy, but Fred and Bobby got on early. I was introduced to the Kennedy women about three or four times each because they couldn't remember my name. After I got to know them, I was more understanding, but at first. . . .

Every Wednesday Senate wives met to fold pieces of gauze into squares. Drove me nuts. If you were the widow of a senator, you could still come back, and those Wednesdays became their link with the outside

John and Wick-kie
Tabbytite, 1956

LaDonna Harris, ca.
1945–46

Fred and LaDonna on
their wedding day, 1949

Left to right:
Grandmother Wick-kie,
mother Lily, LaDonna,
and daughter Kathryn,
1950

Kathryn, Fred, and LaDonna on the
campaign trail, 1964

LaDonna campaigning for Fred,
1964

The Harris family, 1967: Laura,
Fred, LaDonna, Kathryn, Byron

Fred and LaDonna, 1967

Fred and LaDonna during
Hubert Humphrey's
presidential campaign,
1968

LaDonna Harris, ca. 1974–75

LaDonna, campaigning for Fred, 1975

Fred and LaDonna attending a ceremony at Taos Pueblo for the return of Taos Blue Lake, 1978.

LaDonna Harris, 1997

world. We all sat there and made bandages. It was boring as hell. All we did was gossip. I remember the annual luncheon that was sponsored by the Senate wives. The vice president's wife, Muriel Humphrey, was our chair. I came through the reception line with Ethel Kennedy right behind me. She acted like a little girl right out of junior high and said to me, "Kid, who is that?" I said, "Ethel, you have been here longer than I have. How do I know who all these people are? I just got to town, but I'll find out for you." She was more uncomfortable than I was, and I found that very curious. I guess as the attorney general's wife she didn't have to go out publicly, so she stayed very timid. With my lack of skills I wasn't that comfortable myself because it was all a new experience. I remember Ethel asking me where I lived, and I told her. She said, "Well, you live right next to me. How are you going home?" She offered me a ride and since they lived about two long country blocks from us, I accepted. When she dropped me off, she invited us to swim in their pool, and that's how our friendship got started.

The Kennedys had an interesting assortment of friends, from athletes they admired to movie stars. We had a wonderful friendship with them and occasionally flew up to Hyannisport in the family plane to spend the weekend. They were a very competitive family, passing judgment even among themselves on who had the most interesting guest. President Johnson called us once at Hyannisport and said, "Goddammit, Fred, I thought you were my boy. Here you are up there cavorting with those Kennedys, and I just wanted to let you know that I knew where you were." It felt like we were hiding. I think that Johnson and Bobby Kennedy got crosswise in the early part of the administration, but I liked the old rascal. He reminded me of Fred's father when he said, "Goddamm this and Goddamm that, son of a bitch." But although Johnson and Fred could really communicate, to me the Kennedys were just fascinating.

We met all kinds of people through them, particularly Eunice and Sarge Shriver. Sarge was head of the War on Poverty program, and we worked closely with him. He and Eunice, Fritz Mondale, and the founder of Common Cause, John Gardner (I thought the world of him), came to Oklahoma once when Sarge was the head of the Office of

Economic Opportunity (OEO) [also known as the the War on Poverty office]. Bobby Kennedy also visited Oklahoma and we asked all of our Indian people to invite one white person to come and see him. It gave the Indians a sense of their own self-worth and an elevated status among the members of the tribe to ask a white person to join them. Believe it or not, we had whole busloads of people.

I don't know if Senate wives always made bandages, but continuing to fold them was making me crazy, and I really had to do something productive. Muriel Humphrey, Joan Mondale, and I decided to beautify the Capitol because Lady Bird Johnson in 1966 or thereabouts was beautifying the other grounds. The Capitol architect wouldn't let her touch the Capitol grounds. We thought it would be nice to have a restaurant for visitors with a balcony and umbrellas so they could sit outside. We wanted to paint and clean up a little place used by our husbands and their staffs and then use that for our facility, but there was no way the bureaucrats were going to let us get involved. However, we did manage to introduce a new program. Four of us could sew and made baby layettes, diapers, blankets, and nightshirts. They went to servicemen's children in Iceland. Why Iceland, no one knows.

When the troops started coming back from Vietnam in the middle 1960s, we made another article, a little bag to hang on the side of a bed to keep toiletries in. It was khaki green with a little red cross on it. At least I did that. Most of the Senate wives made bandages and gossiped.

MENTAL HEALTH AND RACE

All this time I stayed in touch with folks back home, who remained excited for us. My work with Oklahomans for Indian Opportunity went on and we booked our board meetings when I could travel from Washington to Oklahoma. I deliberately kept that connection. In 1966 the Comanches were moving forward on their separation from the Kiowas and had gotten a constitution written up. Some sort of economic development was high on their list of revenue-generating projects, but that effort didn't get too far. They were also working toward getting back

the Fort Sill Indian School and the lands that had belonged to the tribe but had become agricultural experiment stations.

I remained on the board of the Southwest Center for Human Relations Studies at OU and was still very much involved in race relations and mental health. People seemed to be excited to find a U.S. senator's wife who was interested in mental health, particularly at the time the secretary of Health, Education, and Welfare (HEW), Abe Ribicoff, held hearings on the mental health of children.[5] I was asked to testify, and Fred reminded me to be articulate, saying, "If you're going to talk to members of Congress, you only have five minutes at most before their eyes start glazing over. You don't have two hours to explain Indian programs to Congress." He knew, however, that if I did have two hours, I could do a lot.

Back in 1962 when Abe Ribicoff was head of HEW, I had been asked to serve on a commission focusing on the mental health of children. I agreed and went to the meetings where I became very impressed with another member, Eleanor Roosevelt's daughter (I'm very bad on names). I always believed the mental health professional groups had the answer to racial problems. It was one of the few groups I had up on a pedestal because I believed they were the key to combating the horrible racism that existed. I sat at those meetings and listened and occasionally raised questions through my experiences with OIO and integrating Lawton. The others looked at me in a very patronizing way. All white people, the majority of them were men and I am a woman not of their profession. They must have wondered what I really knew about their field. I raised questions like, "What about children of color?" I used that term and then added, "What we have just discussed as a solution wouldn't apply to Indian children." I suggested that either we talk about it some more or have speakers address us. They usually said, "Oh, LaDonna, you're so nice, but. . . ."

And, of course, being an Indian woman, I knew I was being patronized. I was so frustrated. I liked them individually but they were trapped by their own experiences and couldn't get outside them.

That's when I began to realize that these people didn't know shit about what was happening in this country about race. I was so struck by that. I

complained to Fred over and over again and then suggested that I would like to have them over to the house for a buffet supper. He agreed. I wanted to do it around the time that Iola Hayden and Bill Gover, both American Indians and old friends, were coming to town, whenever that would be, and planned to invite Chester Pierce, also an old friend who was a black psychiatrist from Harvard. Several others were also invited and everyone came.

An interesting dynamic happened at the buffet dinner. We had a few drinks, served food, and then were talking. I said, "Well Chet [Dr. Pierce], why don't you tell them about the things that we discovered together in Oklahoma?" And then I turned to another guest, a sociologist, and said, "Your studies indicate this and that, and these are some of the issues we have talked about in our mental health commission group." I thought that with their professional backgrounds, it would be great.

Iola, who was with OIO, added some commentary as we were going along but poor Bill Gover got drunk because he was so intimidated. It's a wonder I, too, wasn't overwhelmed at that time because I was very sensitive about being undereducated. Bill Gover walked up to one of the people there who was wearing a bolo tie that had a different color stone in it, not turquoise but a stone from Vermont, I believe. Bill grabbed the bolo tie and said, "Just be Goddamm glad that's not turquoise." The man asked why and Bill replied, "Because I'd have to whip your ass, that's why." He was basically telling the other fellow not to patronize him. The hostility he showed just scared the heck out of everybody and they began to recognize that they didn't know very much. Later, I was accused of orchestrating the whole scene. Well, I had no idea what Bill was going to do or how he was going to behave, and I was really embarrassed at the time.

But the combination of the black professionals and the crazy Indian Bill Gover convinced the mental health commission members to have a task force [subcommittee] on the mental health of children of color. They asked me to help them find the members and I suggested Ada Deer, who was a social scientist. We didn't have American Indian psychologists. She

and I were the two Indians working on the subcommittee. There was also a fellow from New Mexico who later became assistant secretary of agriculture, Alex Mercure, and an Hispanic woman from San Francisco. Altogether, there were a total of three Hispanics, two Indians, three blacks, named Chet Pierce, Price Cobbs (who wrote *Black Rage*), and another fellow, and one Puerto Rican, two Jews, one Japanese who was interned in the concentration camp during the war, and I think that's it.

I had the subcommittee members quickly over to my house to socialize them into a group and we all became fast friends. Ada Deer was trying at that time to start a group comprised of Indians working in the many aspects of the social sciences and that's how I got to know her. Price Cobbs thought I was black because Harris is a good black name. He talked street talk to me and then he was embarrassed because he found out I was a senator's wife. He almost died.

During this time Price's book, *Black Rage*, came out. It consisted of individual case histories of what American society had required of blacks, such as straightening their hair, their appearance. It does terrible things to your psyche to change who you are into someone who would be more acceptable. I know all about those feelings because I felt them too, but as a Native American. One story that I remember sticks in my mind. It was about a black soldier stationed in Montana. He got away from the base and drove way up into the mountains to admire the view. When he became hungry he went to a small town for food, parked his car, and walked down the street looking for a restaurant. Everyone came out of the stores and stared at him. He went into a restaurant and asked why people were looking at him. The waitress said, "You are the first black we have ever had in this town, and you'll just have to excuse us for looking at you." He said, "Well, I'd like to have a hamburger," and she said, "I'm sorry but we don't serve blacks."

Our subcommittee concluded that white racism was the number one mental health problem in the country, and it was not only horrible for the ones who were discriminated against, it was as bad or worse for the ones who discriminated. That in itself was a mental health problem because

it was such a negative characteristic. When we presented our findings and conclusions the rest of the group just went ape shit and said, "What do you mean? You can't say this!" But that was our honest conclusion based on discussions among ourselves and research. This happened just before the explosion in civil disorders, right in the 1967–68 period.

The main group, comprised of committee members who were not on our small subcommittee, believed that blacks were taking over, and they began to discredit our minority subcommittee. We fought it and they retaliated by saying we were not professionals. Again, I was the only nonprofessional in the group and two of the black professionals, Chet and Price, thought it was most important not to become discredited, because there were so few black psychiatrists at the time. They were very well known and recognized in their own communities and by their institutions, so they called for a general meeting of all committee members because of all the criticism. At the general meeting we justified our findings. We rationalized, justified, proved, and tried to present our case, but the majority still wouldn't accept it. It was so out of their realm of educational knowledge that they just couldn't go along. They had no experience. They were not working in our field and so they denied our findings and conclusions and wouldn't even put the minority report as an appendix to their report.

SOCIAL SCENE AND FAMILY

Meantime, I was still continuing to meet with and sensitize Sarge Shriver, the head of OEO. As a result, in the mid-1960s we obtained money for OEO programs in Oklahoma that were administered by OIO. A lot of our funding came because of knowing cabinet members and through Lee Udall, the wife of cabinet member Stewart Udall, then secretary of the interior.

Each cabinet member could use the presidential yacht called the Sequoia, so when the Udalls got the opportunity, we were invited to join them for dinner on the yacht. Members of Congress and the cabinet were very close in those days but nowadays they don't do those kinds of things. It's more of a battle today. Back then, we got to know each other

socially and had a whole different working relationship. I remember one cute story, one incident. I found a very charming man on the yacht and we were chatting, so we got our food and sat down together. Fred came by and spoke to me in Comanche. I wondered what was wrong with him, because Fred speaking to me in my native tongue usually signals that something is wrong. Finally it dawned on me that I probably didn't know who the gentleman was. After a while I excused myself and sat beside Fred. He said, "Do you know that you're talking to the head of the CIA?"

Insofar as entertaining was concerned, we had a small house by Virginia and Georgetown standards, so when we had a party we had to take our big dining room table down and put up three small tables to allow our guests to have good conversation. It was natural for me to get acquainted with the staff at the Senate dining room, so I made friends with the maitre d' and the serving staff. No other Senate wife bothered, apparently, but I always enjoyed it because they paid attention to me when I came in. We hired the maitre d' for our parties because he moonlighted on the side. He later wrote a book in which he mentioned that I was one of the few Senate wives he was fond of. He catered our dinners, prepared the meals, and brought them out. Our campaign committee got together and bought us lovely china, silverware, and glassware so we could do this kind of entertaining. To me it was great fun, and when I didn't know enough about the etiquette of it all, I looked it up. Fred was nervous but people loved our parties because they could all get into the conversation. We also socialized with members of the press so they could see that we were serious about our efforts. I am a firm believer in socializing with people so you can bond before you collaborate. Those are some of the things I learned.

I became slowly involved in other social issues in Washington. Fred and I went to receptions practically every night at first and then learned that we should be more selective of who and what interested us, both international or local. These receptions had to have some connection to what we were doing or wanted to learn about.

The three children were with us in Washington and Mary Jackmon from Lawton took care of them. Remember her? I told you that we had asked her to come to Washington with us, live in, and become a member of our family. She had already become practically a surrogate mother, and during the campaign she ran the whole household because I was gone so much. When we asked her father for permission to take her with us, he said, "I know Mary Evelyn can do anything she wants to do, but I am concerned about her little sister, Stella Mae." He was dying from cancer at the time we were planning to leave for Washington and asked us to find a job in DC for Stella as well so he wouldn't have to worry about her. They were the two youngest of his children and everyone else was married and gone out of the household. Not to be married in Oklahoma at their ages was very serious. Fred agreed and said he'd find work for Stella, so she became our receptionist. Mary lived with us and helped Stella find an apartment.

The two sisters live together in Washington now and Laura still stays in touch with them. When she goes to Washington she makes sure there's time to see the sisters. Laura is closer to Mary than Kathryn is, but Kathryn was a teenager at the time we were in Washington. Mary restricted Kathryn somewhat, but they got on well, considering most teenagers are werewolves. Kathryn was a hardworking kid in high school at the time who found her own bunch of friends. Byron's best friend was the son of a doctor who lived right next door to us, and there were certainly enough young people who became Laura's playmates. It was a good neighborhood for everyone.

MORE OPPORTUNITIES

We became closer friends with Sarge Shriver and I mentioned issues to him, saying it wasn't appropriate to deny the Oklahoma tribes OEO funds just because we didn't have a land base. I told him that we still had communities that were being discriminated against, and sending OEO funds through the states was inappropriate because some Oklahoma officials perceived Indian tribes as a threat. I tried to help in that way,

and Sarge then asked me to become an advisor to the War on Poverty. It was an unofficial position, and I was just someone he selected to evaluate some of the programs and provide input. Having come from Lawton, Oklahoma, and having worked on integration, there were a lot of things I had experienced. At that time, Oklahoma was way ahead of other states, but now it's gone backwards.

The War on Poverty gave me a forum and then President Johnson appointed me to the National Indian Opportunities Council. Other members were chairmen of their tribes. There were eight of us and I was the only nonelected official. I told the group that Oklahomans for Indian Opportunity looked at urban issues because there were large numbers of Indians in Tulsa and Oklahoma City, all unorganized. I said we wanted to start Indian centers but were concerned about it because that was separate from our integration efforts. On the one hand we were working for integration, and on the other hand we were working for separatism. We had to deal with those issues and make decisions in our own heads. We learned quite a bit about dropout rates, urban Indian issues, and rural development over in eastern Oklahoma; they were, in relative terms, so underdeveloped.

At that time the Cherokees, Choctaws, Creeks, Chickasaws, and Seminoles in eastern Oklahoma were still run by the BIA. One of them, the Choctaws, was almost terminated, as I've said before. The BIA selected their chairman and it was one of the few tribes in Oklahoma that designated the differences between the full bloods and the "breeds," so to speak. The full bloods were looked down upon by certain BIA sympathizers, if you can imagine that, in the 1950s and early 1960s, because the BIA chose people of mixed blood as their leaders. For example, they chose people like the vice-chairman of Phillips Petroleum, who is an Indian. A few years earlier, when we had visited the Choctaws, they were hauling water because they didn't have wells, or at best had shallow wells. Their general stores were like company stores. While members of Congress like Ed Edmonson and Carl Albert had good reputations, they let the bureau [the BIA] call the shots and were just

keeping the Indians quiet and not wanting them to become a bothersome group.[6] We thought that was horrible. Anyway, that's some of the background I came from into the national situation.

Being on Shriver's board exposed me to other groups of people and because I had done some work in the mental health field, I was asked to be on one of those boards. I was also on the board of the Urban League in Whitney Young's time. Knowing him was fascinating and that's how I came to know the late Ron Brown, former secretary of commerce under President Bill Clinton. Brown was a young attorney then. Then we (a group of activists with similar interests) created the Urban Coalition, which was something John Gardner wanted, because we were having all that racial stress in urban areas. Our task was to figure out ways corporations and neighborhoods could come together to better the community.

At the same time, I had to do all the nice things Senate wives were supposed to do, like fold bandages and be involved in social activities. It was fascinating to me and I shared it all with Fred because he was interested too. We got all kinds of recognition and awards for what we did. *The New York Times* recognized us, as did B'nai B'rith for our civil rights activism. Many times I was the token Indian and token woman on many boards. I realized that and my whole idea was to learn strategies from everyone and create a network of people. That turned out to be quite valuable.

Of course, with Eleanor Roosevelt as my heroine, I could do all these things and be a mother. Yes, be a mother. I don't think I could have done it without Mary Evelyn Blackmon. I tried to do a good job with all my children, and I think I did. Not bragging.

WASHINGTON DC
INSIDERS

6

I'm more radical now than I ever was, but there are only a few people who stayed that way.

In the heyday of the 1960s, when people marched in the streets against the Vietnam War and in favor of women's liberation, when blacks and whites shouted epithets from jail cells, and when painted peace signs filled previously blank urban walls, LaDonna Harris sat beside her husband as he conducted meetings around the country for the Kerner Commission. Assembled by President Lyndon B. Johnson in 1967, the Kerner Commission was also known as the National Commission on Civil Disorders. As we have seen, LaDonna was never a silent partner, but she strengthened her public voice during this unusual time in American history.

~

The blacks on our Mental Health Commission subcommittee quit because they were so outraged at the behavior of the majority. The rest of us stayed on and tried to fight them, but it did no good. Not even a footnote indicated there was another piece of the report, let alone a dissension. We were still looking for solutions. How do you deal with children dropping out of school? How can you improve someone's self-image?

About this time [ca. 1968] all hell broke loose across the country in the area of civil rights. Fred suggested on the floor of the Senate that the government hold hearings and set up a committee to investigate the causes of the disorders. The president agreed, not because of Fred's comments exactly, but because stupid old J. Edgar Hoover said these uprisings were communist-inspired. I saw Hoover's reports, and you just can't imagine how unprofessional they were. They reported things like "a person was seen in the company of someone who was thought to be a communist."

The committee became known as the Kerner Commission.[1] Fred and the mayor of New York, John Lindsey [another commission member], became very effective. They were both politically interested and saw the situation as a major social problem. Fred invited our minority mental health group to testify and we used the term "white racism." That was the first time anyone had ever heard it, so I think we made a major contribution to the Kerner Commission in that way.

The commission staff set up meetings across the country shortly after it was created in 1967, and I went with Fred to visit every city that had a civil rights disturbance. We listened to testimonies nationwide. Some staff went with us, but not another senator. There were only two on the commission, Fred and the black senator from Massachusetts, Edward Brooke, who really didn't pay any attention. Judge Otto Kerner himself wasn't even interested. As I recall, he was being attacked at that time for taking bribes.

When the president first set up the commission, the White House called Fred and told him to listen to the radio one night. Johnson was scheduled to make an announcement, we were told, that would interest Fred. Before the broadcast Laura answered the telephone and was asked, "Is your Daddy there?" That was how the president talked. Fred took the phone and the president said, "Well, Fred, I'm going to do what you suggest and set up the commission. Now you know whose boy you are." Fred saluted and said back to him, "Yessir, Mr. President." Johnson replied, "Fred, you're going to be my boy, aren't you? If I find out that you're not my boy, I'll hunch down and cut your pecker off with my

pocket knife." That's what the president of the United States said. In a room full of staff men and women I asked, "Fred, what did he say?" Fred answered, "Well. . . ." Finally, he told us only that LBJ put him on the commission.

Johnson was afraid that John Lindsey was going to run for president, because he was being mentioned as a possible Republican candidate. John Lindsey may have had political ambitions but he had terrible race riots on his hands in New York that he was trying to keep under control. Johnson telephoned Fred and said, "I hear Lindsey has you down and has his foot on your neck." Fred said, "What?" LBJ said, "My reports are that Lindsey has you down." Fred responded, "No, sir, Mr. President, it's just the opposite. I have to get somebody to help me on this commission." The rest of the members weren't paying attention and of course it was important to have Lindsey's cooperation, being that he was from the largest city in the country then. Fred tried to discuss it rationally with LBJ, but the president didn't want to hear it. Racism was rampant in the country at the time and we learned that labor leaders, for example, came to see the president and said, "What's this about that southern boy, Fred, helpin' all these niggers?" Our liberal position wasn't very popular in certain quarters, including back home in Oklahoma, particularly eastern Oklahoma and several places like that.

After LBJ decided not to run for reelection in 1968, and Hubert Humphrey became the Democratic candidate, Fred and Fritz Mondale were Hubert's campaign managers. During this time Kathryn was at Harvard and was part of the antiwar movement there. Her friends used our house when they were demonstrating in downtown Washington. I remember crying about this at one of the Urban Coalition meetings. Nobody knew what to do with these kids and all this activity. I burst into tears and said that at my house the children came down from Harvard and wrote their telephone numbers on their arms, for example who to contact in case of emergencies, and fixed their gas masks with Vaseline and wet handkerchiefs. We saw them getting ready to go out and be attacked by our own government. Kathryn always had terrible guilt about the fact that the young men had to make decisions regarding

draft dodging, either go to Canada or burn their draft cards. She said it was totally unfair and that women had to take really hard stands but not necessarily ruin their careers or their life experiences over the choice as the men did.

~

Kathryn remembered similarly. "When friends and students came from Harvard to Washington for the peace rallies," she told me, "that were occurring during that period, the late sixties and early seventies, our house would be the base for people who couldn't afford hotel rooms. I remember there were some twenty of us and [other] people with sleeping bags all over the living room. Mother fixed us a big breakfast and then we all went off to the march. A lot of the students were amazed at how responsive and supportive my family was compared to what they were experiencing with their own families. I think I was very blessed in a lot of ways."[2] Kathryn was also blessed in that she was never arrested, partly because she had been alerted by her mother as to the family's experiences with police. At an early age she became wary and street wise. Consequently, the police riot that occurred in Chicago at the 1968 Democratic Convention was no surprise.

While significant to Kathryn, the events in the streets were of less interest to LaDonna and Fred than those in political backrooms, for Fred was being considered by Hubert Humphrey, the Democratic Party's nominee for president of the United States, as his running mate. Fred's liberal politics were appealing to the political brokers at the time, as was his geographical base, Oklahoma. And there was no doubt that he could be a formidable addition to the Democratic ticket. With his air of confidence and his lawyer's ability to articulate the issues, Fred Harris seemed an ideal candidate. LaDonna recalled that dramatic moment in August 1968 when they were awaiting Humphrey's decision.

~

We were in our rooms, sitting on the window edge, looking at the park, watching all the activity below, and crying. Hubert had Ed Muskie in one room and Fred in the other and was running back and forth because he couldn't make up his mind. He loved them both so much, for one thing, but had he chosen Fred, it would have been a whole

different situation. Unfortunately, Ed Muskie was selected. Still, Hubert Humphrey remained absolutely my favorite human being in the Senate, a most thoughtful person. He was against the war but couldn't do anything about it because of our national policy at that time.

THE COMMISSION CONCLUDES

Hot summer, no jobs—Watts, Harlem, Chicago, Miami, and Detroit. As part of the Kerner Commission, we visited all the towns that had riots in 1968 and held group hearings. Individuals testified, but it was the group response that was so significant, and it became apparent that the slightest incident erupted into violence. In one city, a National Guard member got nervous standing under a street light so he shot off his gun at the light and everybody opened up firing. A mother and child were killed in their home. The killings were stupid and senseless and nobody knew how to handle the situation.

The Kerner Commission final report was ready to go but the *Washington Post* got hold of an advance copy and published it before LBJ saw it and even before the members of the Commission got a chance to present it to the President and discuss the rationale behind it. Johnson read it in the newspaper and got his nose all out of joint. Instead of promoting Fred as the main author, he got mad and stormed off. By that time, they made a deal with a publisher to put it out and so it hit the streets just as soon as it became public. It became part of our culture. Thirty years later, Fred and Roger Wilkins still ask, "Are we really better off?" Nobody seems interested anymore.

The Kerner Commission recommendations became the law of the land and certainly influenced society. Articles and books like Price Cobbs's *Black Rage* became acceptable. I remember that Price asked Fred to write the Foreword and he agreed.[3] Fred had already written several books at that time, and he thought his books would take off and poor old Price's book wouldn't. Well, Price's book was one of the few books of its kind and it has become a classic. There had been a book written back in the 1930s and then James Baldwin wrote, but there were so few that talked about being black, slavery, and all the forms of

discrimination. The time for Price's book was right; the Martin Luther King tragedy and others were happening at the same time.

INDIAN LAND CLAIM BATTLES

In the midst of all this activity in the 1960s, I was still traveling back and forth to Oklahoma where I was the president of OIO. I also was serving on the Urban League and Urban Coalition boards and was advising the War on Poverty program.

I was one of the first Senate wives to testify before Congress and didn't realize that I was setting an historical precedent. I spoke on the need for keeping the War on Poverty programs funded. When Sarge Shriver asked me to testify, at first I said, "Well, I don't know. Let me talk to Fred." Fred said, "Well, OK, if you practice real hard and don't embarrass me." He helped me prepare my statement and when I was in the chamber, Carl Albert came over personally to be there and make sure no one was mean to me. I was just getting out of my stoic period and into my verbal period, so I wasn't quite comfortable yet. And then I'm so dyslexic. Can't read a speech. I knew what I wanted to say and Fred put it in bullet form so I could remember what I wanted to insert. I got through it very well, and then I received a bouquet of two dozen roses from Sarge Shriver. The card read, "To the lady that made the House a home for the poor."

Our next big effort was to help the Taos Pueblo Indians retrieve sacred property, their Taos Blue Lake.[4] The Taos Indians came to Washington to talk to Fred and he asked me to sit in on it after he heard that they wanted to get their sacred Blue Lake back. When they left he said to all of us, "By God, if we don't do anything else in the Senate, we're going to help those folks." Senator Scoop Jackson from the State of Washington was chairman of the Interior Committee at the time and all Indian legislation had to come from there. Scoop opposed the Taos people getting their lake back, but only because Senator Clinton Anderson did and Anderson was Scoop's mentor or idol, you could say. Anderson was a powerful senator from New Mexico. Luckily, Fred devised a strategy that we hoped would work.

We used to have all the White House Fellows over to our house for an evening with us, including supper. Fred would talk about the Senate and I'd talk about Indians and civil rights in general. One member of this group was Bobbie Green, who later married Bill Killberg. We all went to the wedding. Darn if she didn't adopt me because I paid attention to her and was interested in her. She later was assigned to the White House to work for Len Garment, the president's lawyer. She got me into the White House.

President Nixon had come to New Mexico in 1969 or so to meet with the Taos people and had his picture in the paper during his campaign. It was a big vote getter. I reminded all of Nixon's people about it and said, "You used all the Taos people in our campaign and got elected, so I think you might be interested in helping them. We would like to make the return of Blue Lake a nonpartisan effort. We see it as civil rights, human rights, and an Indian rights issue."

After several telephone calls we had a bipartisan meeting in Fred's office, planned some strategies, and let it be known that the White House was interested in the bill. The White House had done something else Scoop Jackson didn't like and he was very upset with them to begin with, but then he found out that they had endorsed the Taos Blue Lake issue, which he and Clinton Anderson had opposed. He was really mad, but we had gotten everyone so involved by that time that nobody could back out.

We brought together a coalition of organizations that had never gotten together before. I started working with all the civil rights groups and convinced labor to talk about it as a human rights issue. We got support from the black community; many groups passed resolutions for us, but darned if the Sierra Club didn't come out against us on this one.

We had the votes in committee to get it out and we knew we had it on the floor, but getting it out of Anderson's Interior Committee was the hardest. Anderson approached Fred on the floor and said, "By God, Fred, I don't mess with your Indians in Oklahoma and you shouldn't mess with mine in New Mexico." Fred just said, "Well, Senator, they're not your Indians." Oh, they got mad at each other over this. Fred just fought the

pants off him in the committee. We had the votes, but we had to count on Senator George McGovern. He came from South Dakota, a big Indian state, but didn't want to cross old man Anderson and Scoop Jackson, too. That would be going against real power. As a consequence, Anderson held up everything from coming out of the Interior Committee for about a month. Even if our issue lost in the committee, we could still take it to the floor for a vote. But Anderson held other pieces of legislation, until finally he let it out. On the day before that, the New Mexico Sierra Club put a flyer on everybody's desk stating that returning the Taos sacred lake was not a good idea. We called around the country and convinced several other Sierra Clubs to go on record to state that the New Mexico Sierra Club wasn't authorized to speak for all the clubs, so we were able to counteract their lobbying effort. [When the vote came] I was sitting up in the balcony of the Senate with the Taos people who were wearing their J. C. Penney blankets. They looked so beautiful. Our bill passed with more than enough votes.

It was a major, major victory, and President Nixon nursed it for all it was worth. At a White House bill signing, there were Indians all over the room. Right before the president signed it, he looked up and said, "I can't believe I'm signing a bill that was sponsored by Fred Harris."

The Taos Indians have honored us several times. That was our most exciting endeavor. The people had been fighting for years to get back their lake. It was a lifetime fight for most of the people and it meant so much to them. It is part of their creation myth. They came from Blue Lake.

Our next big fight was the Alaskan claims. I played a major role with the White House in getting the human rights and civil rights people involved. Fred did all the maneuvering on the floor and in the committee. By this time my activities seemed so natural. Trying to help wasn't anything out of the ordinary.

The problem had begun when the United States bought Alaska from the Russians and never settled what land was Indian and what land was non-Indian. When oil was discovered, corporations made plans to produce and exploit the oil, but a little band of Eskimos from the

farthest point of the United States (I'm very bad on names and there are about 125 bands of Eskimos, I think) filed a lawsuit and said, "Just a minute. You can't start production until we get the land issue settled because you may be taking some of our oil."⁵ The Eskimos held the whole thing up and went into court demanding that the issue be settled. The White House recommended a settlement of seven million acres and some money, millions of dollars.

Well, here comes a representative from the northern slopes that said, "We are a subsistence people. We live off the land. A large land base is more important to us than the dollar." Fred then introduced legislation for sixty million acres and some money.

The worst part about it was the liberal lawyers in Washington who represented the tribe. Their own lawyers got really pissed off at Fred because they were going to settle for ten million acres, having talked the administration up from seven to ten. They thought they had really made a coup and were also settling for cash and the corporations to invest the monies. The Eskimos weren't satisfied and told Fred they didn't know how to deal with their lawyers. We stayed with it, working in the same kind of nonpartisan way, and got the Eskimos forty million acres. The senators from Alaska were mad, too, because they didn't want to give up that much acreage to Eskimos. In the meantime, they took away the Eskimos' right to be tribes and set up corporations that included them. We should have known there would be some sort of reaction, but nonetheless, obtaining that large parcel of land was another big success.

Our next big success was with the Menominees, as I described earlier. The concept of termination came out of the 1950s during the Eisenhower administration, if I'm correct.⁶ I remember it as a policy that developed from a paper written by someone at the Brookings Institution.⁷ The idea was based on a theory of assimilation. Because the government couldn't make farmers out of us Indians (we were still acting like Indians) the next step was to just terminate the tribes. Then the people would have to fit in. I understand that Eisenhower himself didn't like the idea, but somebody in power liked it well enough that they initiated it. Relocation also came out of that era.⁸ It was again taking us away from our culture

and our setting. Most of the federal Indian policy has been to make us go away so we would no longer be Indians. In the 1950s we Indians were supposedly fading away so rapidly that there wouldn't be Indians around much longer and this process was designed to help it along. Little did they know that fifty years later we are growing bigger and bigger.

OUR DAUGHTERS´ BATTLES

During these times I had a desk in Fred's office and I would go to work on issues, helping politically, especially if we had evening functions. Of course, Mary took care of the children, who were all in school. She occasionally had dinner waiting for them but most of the time we were home for dinner.

We all had important conversations over dinner. I had become a little more oral and articulate and had to moderate the table. Between Fred and the kids, they wanted to talk about all kinds of subjects. For instance, Kathryn thought we should go to jail to support a case about an Indian-black woman who had married a white guy. Miscegenation was still illegal at the time in Virginia and Kathryn thought she and I should go to jail because we were Indians and my marriage to Fred was illegal. Byron was really upset and asked, "You mean you and Daddy aren't married?" Me in jail? A senator's wife? That would really make news and it would help the litigants and show how foolish this case was. I told Kathryn she was absolutely right and we should look into it.

Kathryn was always upset about Senator Harry Byrd, the senator from Virginia, because he was so conservative. She once asked Fred if it would embarrass him if she became involved in fighting the Byrd machine. She organized against Byrd when he was still very strong and very popular in the Senate. When any legislation arose that we absolutely could not tolerate, she and I threatened to lie down in the driveway so that Fred couldn't go to Congress unless he agreed to vote our way. We had learned all these tactics in the civil rights movement. Kathryn just fascinated me in what she listened to and what she absorbed.

Laura, on the other hand, always got in trouble in school because she stood up for those who weren't popular with the teacher. She went to a

private day care and they used her as kind of a teacher's aide right from the start. Ethel Kennedy's nephew also went to that school and had terrible behavior problems after the plane crash that killed his parents. Teachers couldn't coax him into behaving properly, but Laura could. She was so effective with him that they allowed her to do what she could.

She always took up with somebody and argued with her teachers in class. I remember that we got a horrible note from her first grade teacher that asked us to come in and talk with them. One note said, "You may think she's cute, but she is terrible. She disrupts the children and then they all follow her and do what she does." We talked with her about it. Here she was, a first grader who had been in school only two months and was already having trouble in school. I asked Fred to go with me to talk with the teacher because if he didn't I might get so mad that I'd cry and it wouldn't do us any good at all. At school, Fred took the offensive and said, "I just can't imagine how this could come about that you cannot manage a first grader who was so excited about coming to school. She comes home with stomachaches and doesn't like school at all." He chewed the poor teacher out and she burst into tears, admitting this was the first class she had ever taught. Fred backed up a little bit at that. I asked, "Can't we find a good way to solve this? If you don't like her, then we probably should make some other kinds of arrangements." Well, I came to find out that Laura wasn't telling us everything. She had also been tied into her seat. When she dropped a pencil on the floor and got out of her chair to pick it up, the teacher tied her into her seat and told her not to get out of her chair because every time she did, all the other children did too.

~

Laura remembered another aspect of her younger years in school. "I always got in trouble," she said, "for challenging my teachers, usually because of their lack of knowledge on a subject or their racist or sexist statements and attitudes."[9] LaDonna recalled a specific situation.

~

Another incident had to do with a young Cuban girl in the class who was having difficulty with the language. Laura befriended her. The teacher

announced to the class that the girl was retarded, and it really made Laura mad. She said, "She is not retarded. She speaks a different language and she thinks differently." Laura got into a big argument with the teacher because she took the side of the Cuban girl. When Kathryn was about the same age, she got in a fight over evolution with a neighbor who was a deacon in the church. She was nine years old when she told him that evolution had occurred and he told her it hadn't. That ruined our neighborhood relationship, but it was the way the kids were brought up. [My children] were always involved in things, not overly managed, free spirits.

REPRESENTING URBAN INDIANS

Although Washington DC is an international city, and its environs house families and individuals from all over the globe, the mix of ethnic backgrounds in the 1960s excluded significant political representation of the Indian population in the city. Naturally, once LaDonna discovered the omission, she wanted to remedy that situation.

~

When we got to Washington, nobody was talking about urban Indians. The occupation of Alcatraz hadn't occurred yet, but the American Indian Movement (AIM) announced there were urban Indians in need of services.[10] Don't forget, Indians were forced to live in cities because of the government's urban relocation policy. Back home I started focusing on urban Indian problems because it was part of a turf situation.

My emphasis started in Oklahoma because we had a large Indian population in Tulsa and Oklahoma City who weren't receiving any of the War on Poverty programs that LBJ had set up. We wondered how to best serve those people. Was it to set them up in separate organizations? That would be going back to segregation. We were working for integration on the one hand, and then we were acting as Indians and setting up separate institutions as Indians. At first I saw it as a conflict, but it really wasn't. We decided we had to do it this way [as separate entities] and then when people got stronger they could do all the other things.

President Johnson had said he would do two things: put an Indian in charge of the Bureau of Indian Affairs and pass the Indian Preference Agreement. I was there in the middle 1960s when he appointed Bob Bennett, an employee of the BIA, who was originally from Wisconsin. Johnson said, "We want everybody to know that the Department of the Interior does not own Indians. Indians are full American citizens and they should have as much access to all the federal programs as any other citizen." It was a fine speech. Johnson then said to Bennett, "I know there's a lot of dead wood in the BIA. You go to the Smithsonian and get you a damn tommyhawk and just knock the hell out of all that dead wood. Get something done." That's the way the president spoke.

In Washington I started to branch out, particularly after Lyndon Johnson set up the National Indian Opportunities Council, one of the Great Society programs specifically designed to open access to employment of Indians. He appointed me to be a member. Peter McDonald [former chairman of the Navajo Tribe] was the chair. When Nixon became president, he loved us Indians too, so he kept up the council and appointed someone from Occidental Petroleum. We taught him real fast. Bill Carmack, from Stewart Udall's staff, was another appointee, as were Wendell Chino, from the Mescalero Apache Reservation, and Roger Jourdain. Sorry, but I can't remember the rest of them.

I was the only non-elected official on the council, and I think my appointment was a recognition of both the fact that I was a senator's wife and was coming into my own. A combination of both, much like those mental health days. And, Johnson liked women. I was still head of a statewide organization, OIO, and was becoming visible in the War on Poverty program. Then too, I knew all the White House staff. My area of interest at the time was urban Indians and I held hearings on the subject all over the country: Los Angeles, San Francisco, Minneapolis, St. Paul, and Dallas. I remember working with Vine DeLoria too.[11] At that time he was head of the National Congress of American Indians.[12]

The hearings were fascinating. For example, I was told that in Dallas there were only about twelve hundred urban Indians in all of the city. I had chosen Dallas because I knew the old relocation program had

affected them there. I said, "I have more relatives than that down here. Comanches and other tribal people are related to me." As a senator's wife, I went to the Dallas mayor's office and he assigned somebody to work with me. It was a big deal, a presidential commission, and I had fun. I met with a few Indian people at first and then they brought all kinds of people in. I had my Comanche kin folks there to organize the hearing and we did a great job. It was a big story.

In San Francisco there were two major Indian groups, one in the Oakland area and one in San Francisco itself. We had to bring them all together in order to have a hearing on urban problems. We couldn't have a hearing in one place or another because one or the other group would get pissed off; they bitched about everything. Finally, we decided to hold the hearing in a hotel. Representatives from the Indian communities told us about police brutality, in particular, and how many people were in jail.

I thought it was a very profound meeting. After it was over, people complained that we on the hearing staff hadn't gone to any of the centers, so I suggested we start on Mission Street in San Francisco. We all piled into a car, the five staff members and me. When we got there, we walked down Mission Street, an ugly old bar street.

The Indians and the Samoans in the neighborhood had been fighting each other over women. Apparently the Samoans were dating some Indian women and the Indian men didn't like it. I didn't know about that particular problem because it hadn't been part of our discussions at the hearing. The main talk there had been about arrests and what the city was or wasn't doing.

So here I was, in the Mission area of town. We parked our car and walked past some of the bars. One had an opening right onto the street and inside was an Eskimo woman who had testified during the hearings. She called to me, took me into the bar, and offered to buy me a drink. I couldn't have refused. We stood close to the door because we were on our way to an Indian center with a fellow named Oakes, a leader of the urban group. He and his friend, a Sioux woman, became part of our entourage. (It was they who had suggested that we go to the Mission area.)

Oakes stood up on a barstool and hollered, "Hey, everybody, LaDonna Harris is here. She's a Comanche and her husband is a senator." When he hopped down, all the people crowded in and we shook hands all around. One minute he was standing right by me and the next minute, when I turned around, all of a sudden he was on the floor. Here come the Samoans, and they knocked the heck out of him.

Everyone started moving around and a big fight broke out, right between the door and us. One of the Indian staff people yelled to me, "Let's get you out of here. We can't have you involved in a bar fight. Let's try the back door." Of course, it was locked, which was against the law. The staff people pushed me up to the bar and stood around me to protect me. Everybody was fighting at that time. Pretty soon, the bartender (he didn't call the police) got up on top of the bar with a big bat and yelled, "Goddammit, you stop that fighting! The police are on the way. I'm going to beat the shit out of all of you!" I looked around and saw a guy with a knife and a barstool leg.

I have been in lots of places but never in a place like that. It was frightening. The Indians finally threw the Samoans out and everybody then re-congregated to find out who was hurt. In the entire ruckus, somebody snatched the purse of the Sioux woman who was with me. Another person lost a big old silver watch. It got pulled off him. A Delaware Indian from Oklahoma who was going to school there at the University of California had been wearing a clip-on tie, which he lost. After it was all over we made so much fun of him. Here everybody was losing valuables and he lost his tie! I was so shaken, shaken to my core. I could have been seriously hurt.

We then went over to the Mission Indian Center and didn't have much of a discussion, just refreshed ourselves. The boys got the car, drove it right up front, and I got in. But right before that, as we walked out of the Indian Center onto the street and were fixing to get into the car, along came a police car. The officer called, "Are you alright?" or something like that. The Sioux woman yelled back, "You sons of bitches. Where were you when we needed you?" and started to cuss them out. They jumped out of the car and said, "Listen here, lady, watch it." I tried to intervene

and said, "She's very upset." Then she told the policeman that I was a United States senator's wife who almost got killed in a bar fight. She sounded like a blabbering idiot. They said, "We don't care who she is. If you can't stop being so abusive, we'll run you in."

That's exactly what always happens. The police never come on the street and break up any fights if you call them. They just let the Indians fight. And then they'd come late at night and arrest them, put them all in the drunk tank. Things like this are what the Indians testified to at the hearings, and I got to see it for myself. My staff wrote a letter to Mayor Joseph Alioto and we got five letters of apology from him and from the chief of police, and from everybody else. They finally made some changes, though.

Anyway, the staff people took me back to the hotel, and the lone woman on the staff was just as shaken, so she went to the room with me. We sat for a minute and talked about what happened and how frightened we were. Then she left and went to her room to bed.

All of a sudden Fred Harris appeared from clear across the country. I didn't know he was coming. Up to that point and way into our relationship we had never been away from each other for more than two nights and then we'd call each other every night. I started to tell Fred about what happened and he became very angry because he thought I had embarrassed him. Poor fellow. He had been smoking four packs of cigarettes a day but now he said to me, "You haven't even noticed that I quit smoking, and I can't stand it." He was so messed up and couldn't do it by himself so he had flown out to California.

Well, between the combination of events, I felt like I had been slapped around, but good things came out of all that. In particular, I'm talking about my organization, Americans for Indian Opportunity.[13]"

ACTIVISM

7

To live in this world, I have to take a deep breath.

As a result of the National Opportunities Council hearings, LaDonna was able to attract more money into the Indian communities. At the same time, a leading political organization, the National Congress of American Indians, lost its volatile director, Vine DeLoria Jr., and nothing appeared exciting to LaDonna in Indian country. That is usually a time when all sorts of adventurous ideas pop into her head. For a while she had been thinking of expanding the concept of Oklahomans for Indian Opportunity to encompass a national perspective. In 1970, when the lull in Indian country activity occurred, the time suddenly seemed right. The first effort was to raise money.

~

When we started AIO, Fritz Mondale introduced a financial genius, Herb Allen, to Fred, and we became friends fast; he made a major donation to AIO. We visited him at his Long Island, New York, big old house that overlooked the river. We flew with him in his Lear jet and vacationed with him in Latin America and the islands. The Ford Foundation also

gave us start-up money and we held fund-raisers in Washington and New York City in the early 1970s.

At our Washington event, a group of Kiowa dancers and notable Indians appeared: Floyd Westerman, Ada Deer, Joe Dan Osceola from Florida, Joe Sando (the board member with the most years of service and still going strong) from Jemez Pueblo and Alma Patterson (the first Indian social worker in the nation) from the Tuscarora tribe. A lot of people came to the fund-raiser just to see Indians. I remember some of the movie people who came, for example Candace Bergen and Ray Stark, who brought Barbra Streisand.

Andrew Stein at that time was on the City Council of New York and was a real up-and-coming politician. He attached himself to Fred, so we asked him to have a fund-raiser for us out in the fancy Hamptons of Long Island. He agreed, and Fred told him how to set it up, but he wouldn't do it that way. Those were the days of the radical chic. At the function I met Gloria Steinam for the first time. The famous designer, Vera, produced a scarf for us; I still have a couple that I put away somewhere. Bill Gover got drunk again, but this time he didn't embarrass me. I wish I had had the personality to have done something about him, but at that time I wasn't strong enough. Because it was in East Hampton, New York, we invited the Shinnecocks to join us.[1]

Fund-raising was one of the worst things I have ever done in my life. I promised I would never put myself in that position ever again. We hardly raised any money at all, hardly covered expenses, just because Stein didn't listen to Fred teaching him about fund-raising. That was one of our negative experiences, but we learned from it. The celebrities were just there to be seen, not to get anything done or raise any money. They weren't quite sure they wanted to do that, so I met with some of them in advance of the reception. They stayed. Everything about that experience, except meeting the Shinnecocks, was just repugnant to me.

BALANCING ACT

Also in the line of fund-raising for AIO, I had gone to the Equitable Life Insurance Company in New York in 1970 and made an appointment to

see the president. Darned if he didn't get the whole board and officers of the company to meet with me. It was intimidating. I wasn't all that well versed at the time and I had to carry most of the conversation. Equitable at that time was run by a bunch of little old men who were like the deacons of a church. It was a different kind of corporate culture. Everybody looked to the president to say something; he was the CEO. Nobody said a thing. Finally the president asked me if I had ever gone to the churches for funding. I said we had but that they didn't understand us and were part of our problem. I went on making my pitch. He didn't know what to say, so he tried to make conversation and show some knowledge. He asked me if I knew there were Indians in New York, and I answered by telling him that there were urban Indians in cities everywhere. He then asked me if I knew that Indians had the innate ability to do high metalwork. I said that I knew that the Mohawks had done steelwork. He said that [walking on high beams] was a quality that they were born with. I said, "yessir." By that time I was pissed off because I had put up with so much.

He continued on, saying, "They just get up there and they have balance and can do all of the work. They're born with it." I said I didn't think so and asked him how he thought they came to be steelworkers. He said, "Well, because I guess they climb trees." Everyone gasped, and the air went dead. I said, "Well, sir, I think you'll find out that companies don't insure those people, and those are the only jobs the Indians can get, a high risk, uninsured job is the real history generation after generation." Then I thanked him for listening to us, dismissed him, and left.

I can't describe the feelings I had. Talk about shuffling! I felt like an Oklahoma whore on the streets of New York—worse, the humiliation was so awful. God, I hated it.

About three months later I had gotten a little money for AIO from here and there, and then a phone call came from the vice-president of Equitable, Coy Eklund. He asked me to have lunch with him, a special lunch. He said he had been out of town on the day I made my presentation, but wanted to meet with me. I went to lunch with him and discovered he had a personal interest. "My father just died," he

said, "and when he came to this country he learned to speak Ojibwe before he spoke English. His best friends were Ojibwe people who helped him through the winter.[2] They came to our house to see my father all the time. Sometimes they just sat and talked. I don't think my mother appreciated them because she sure didn't want us hanging around with Indian kids." When he grew up, Coy worked his way up through Equitable and became the vice-president. He said when his father became ill with cancer he tried to see more of him and read to him. His father said, "What makes me feel so bad is that some of my Ojibwe friends don't speak English. I wish I could figure out some way to help them." Well, I don't know how Coy did it, but he found some old Ojibwe woman that his father had known, visited with her, talked for a long time, got all the sounds down, and then wrote an Ojibwe dictionary. It was a long-distance relationship too. Periodically he went out to visit her, but usually just wrote to her. They developed a system of communication with each other through writing. She cleaned up his language. She was educated as well and a speaker. She knew about phonics but they didn't use phonics. They went by their own sound and created it.

This is what he wanted to tell me and said, "In memory of my father, I'm doing this. You may not believe it, but I am very interested in Indian people and have a relationship with them." We put him on AIO's board immediately and he became our token white person, a corporate white Republican board member. We got support from several other corporations because of Coy. It was impressive to quite a few people that Equitable and Coy were supporting us.

After that he fell madly in love with me, and we have always had a weird kind of affection for each other. A love affair, understood, and just there. He came to all of our board meetings, held luncheons for us in Equitable's executive dining room. Then he became the CEO of Equitable, so I was permitted to invite people to the dining room and raise funds there. I vividly remember looking out the window on the forty-fifth or forty-ninth floor and seeing the Hudson River and Statue of Liberty down below. I involved him in the Urban League and that's

where he and Vernon Jordan met. Vernon put him on the Urban League board, but Coy gives me all the credit. At that time Equitable had a black on its board, they promoted blacks, brought black executives in, and then Coy got involved in the women's movement as well. He promoted women and concluded that it was easier bringing blacks in than it was bringing women in.

To this day Coy continues to be one of my dearest friends. We talk at least once a month. When his wife died he remarried, but people thought he and I should have tied the knot. I said, "Well, I love him but I don't want to marry him." He has been one of the most precious friends I have had throughout my life. Just as an example of what friends can do for friends, he would send his car to pick us up at the airport and when we stayed over, he got us theater tickets. He also had a video studio and taped interviews with me and different members of the Indian community.

Along with Coy on AIO's board, we wanted to constitute it in terms of regions and in terms of Indian populations, such as Joe Dan Osceola from Florida and Philip Martin from Mississippi and Gene Crawford, a Sioux, who was head of the urban center in Omaha, Nebraska. Gene was our vice president for years even though he had a sleeping disorder, an awful sickness. He weighed about three hundred pounds but could carry it because he was so tall. He could drink a fifth of Scotch, eat a lot of food, and then fall asleep right in the middle of the conversation. Once a doctor hosted a gathering for Fred and we were telling Gene Crawford stories. The doctor corrected us, said we shouldn't be laughing, that the disease was very dangerous. He took Gene to Stanford where they did some tests on him and finally put a valve in his throat to keep it from closing when he went to sleep. It's the kind of disease, I believe, that contributes to crib death. Anyway, it didn't mess up his personality, though. We had so much fun! I never saw anyone live life like he did. He did good works all the time.

The first time I saw Gene was at a conference in Omaha. In the lobby of the hotel he had Russell Means by the nape of the neck and was shaking him like a dog, saying, "Russell, Goddamn you, I have helped you do everything you have ever done, and you are bad-mouthing

me." Russell answered, "No, Gene, it wasn't me. I didn't do it." He was apologizing all over the place. I was so impressed because Russell himself was so intimidating and was supposed to be such a rough guy. Crawford just wheeled him around, again and again. He was really a big old teddy bear, so gentle, an ex-marine who had wonderful qualities, who loved old people and got on so well with them. If it hadn't been for the start-up money he and others gave us, we wouldn't have been able to function.

All of our initial board members were chairmen, movers and shakers in their areas, cutting-edge people from all over the country that I either learned about or were recommended to me. The famous Oklahoma ballerina, Maria Tallchief, was one of our board members, as were the social worker Alma Patterson, the actress Candace Bergen, and Willy Hinsley and Ray Stark. They were all eager to help. Incidentally, we have always had an Alaskan board member. To entice them to serve, I just telephoned and said that I felt there was a vacuum in leadership and we needed a national organization, based on what we learned and what came out of our Oklahoma experiences with OIO.

The timing was great. It was the beginning of the 1970s with the social, civic, and human rights movements taking place. Soon after that the Native American Rights Fund was organized and there was a flourish and fermenting of good ideas and wonderful activities in Indian country. There was a need for us to get together, and people saw it. We had been so isolated.

The movement can get in front of you, like the Civil Rights movement. It certainly was during that period of time. Then I had obvious contacts with federal agencies because President Johnson had put me on the National Indian Opportunities Council. So I had access to power. And then I was married to Fred, so I had contacts with a lot of influential people, to put it in the raw sense. Mostly contacts that I learned how to use. Here was this country girl from Oklahoma learning how to use all this. Finally, since I was everybody else's token Indian woman board member, I learned skills and techniques from the other boards I served on. I brought them to AIO's board and expanded the consciousness of Indians as well. It was an exciting time.

ON THE CAMPAIGN TRAIL AGAIN

At the time we were beginning AIO, back in 1970, Grandpa had died in Oklahoma, but Grandma was much alive and living with my mother. I had rented out my house in Lawton, but we had a house in Norman. However, it was really disconcerting to go back and forth from Washington to Oklahoma so much. When we would be back home for short periods, Fred looked at all of his mail and made notes as to how they should be answered. The staff in Washington went through the necessary processes to respond to constituents by mail once we returned to the capital. The majority of our staff was from Oklahoma, and so they were pretty savvy.

Meantime, Fred was enjoying two years of Kerr's term (1964–65) and then had six years on his own. In 1971 he ran on the Democratic ticket for president of the United States, but before he made his decision he asked me what I thought. We talked about it and wrote down the pros and cons. It was a major decision and we thought of it as a great adventure. Lack of money forced us from the race before the primaries. Four years later we again launched a bid for the presidency, this time running in a down-to-earth style we called "new populism." As I look back, I would never consider a presidential campaign now, recognizing all the work that has to go into it.

We concentrated most of our energies in New England, where the first primaries were held, but after poor showings in New Hampshire and Massachusetts primaries, we backed out. We didn't have big corporation financing because we had always been fighting corporate America. Candidates spend whatever it takes to get elected and what it takes is money that we didn't have and couldn't raise. Our volunteers slept on the floor in storefronts and many of them cooked and worked in the snow. It was craziness.

We stayed in peoples' homes and carried our own bags to show that we weren't a pampered part of society. Jimmy Carter later adopted that style. I ran into trouble because I am allergic to cats, so we always had to stay in a place where there weren't any cats. But, besides not having enough resources to make it all, our problem was that we were openly

against the war and had a reputation built on the conclusions of the Kerner Commission. People in many states, Oklahoma included, hadn't really accepted either one. We were so engrossed in what we were doing that we didn't go back home often enough. We could have done it but it would have taken so much energy.

I missed Oklahoma and my family, particularly my grandmother, who had loved the campaign for the presidency. She was getting a little too fragile to take her on the trail with us, so we kept her informed back in Oklahoma. By that time, 1976, Kathryn had been married to Manuel Tijerina. They tied the knot out at the Deyo Mission Church in Oklahoma. Secret Service workers were all around, but Fred really didn't want them. He felt it was too cumbersome and said, "Secret Service can't do anything but keep drunks away and hurt your feelings." Naturally, he wasn't the most popular candidate with them, but once they came along with us, they fell in love with us, and we all became very good friends. They attended Kathryn's wedding along with Kathryn's friends from Harvard and Stanford and Manuel's friends from Stanford and his parents and some of our black friends who helped us integrate Lawton.

Deyo was an Indian church, sitting out there on the prairie. Our regular Comanche pianist was sick that day, so we recruited one of our black friends to take her place. Uncle Robert Coffey, one of the Comanches we worked with in the past, was the minister who performed the services in Comanche and English. We used my great-aunt Rose's house to dress in and when we went outside and she saw the Secret Service, she asked, "Who are those men?" She thought they were bill collectors. In Comanche they are called "people who are always looking for you" because they had suits on! Historically, the Comanches used the same term for the Texas Rangers. A whole bunch of my tribal sisters made Kathryn's wedding dress. It was originally a Vogue pattern, but we Comanche-ized it with beads, a shawl, and the little Comanche dip [shape of the neckline]. The Comanche churchwomen fixed lunch for us and we had a big cake. One of the Secret Service said, "We've done a lot of things in our time, but this [Comanche] wedding takes it."

My grandmother and my mother were there but Mother was in pretty bad shape. She had what we know now as Alzheimer's. The doctors then diagnosed it as hardening of the arteries. When my mother started getting forgetful, she was still young, younger than I am today. She seemed to be having difficulty in her work and in remembering things. She had retired earlier and perhaps shouldn't have. Sister took her to a doctor here in New Mexico who said she was just getting old. Well, she was too young to get old. I took her to Washington where they ran a few tests. My doctor said it was a rapid deterioration and hardening of the arteries. There was diminished flow of blood to the brain and it caused her death.

Grandmother survived my mother and was much more alert and agile than mother had been. We estimated that my grandmother was about eighty-seven to ninety when she died. She fell and broke her hip and might have lasted longer, had that not happened. She always said, "I want to die in the Comanche way." When you're not useful among my people, you are supposed to go off and die. A few months after the accident, she decided she would die and she did, but not before she had outlived all her children. She had lived long enough to see all her children die.

I was talking with a friend recently who is now into home care for people who don't need special care all the time. He just started the business around 1996, and it's growing by leaps and bounds. I told him about my best friend's mother, who died from osteoporosis at age ninety-three. She was all bent over. He wanted to make a pact with me after I told him what the Comanches did. He said, "Let's go up into the mountains to die instead of just hanging around." That's how I feel.

Grandmother hammered it into us. Papa would tell stories, too, about old people who just went off. Back then you couldn't be a burden on the tribe. If you couldn't travel and the enemy was chasing you, or you were such a burden on your family that you endangered them, that was the basis for it. That horrible movie *A Man Called Horse* was really about Comanches, but they said it was the Cheyennes or one of the northern tribes so they could film the Sun Dance. There was a poor

old grandmother in it who went around begging. No Comanche would allow that.

How to die is an individual's decision to make, and everyone has a right to do that. I'm either going to have to develop my Comanche skills in that area or make an appointment with Dr. Kevorkian. I'm not going to lie around in a hospital bed waiting to die.

SPREADING WINGS

8

It's one thing to have all this high technology and be a leader of the world, but if some of your people don't have a quality of life, then what is the good of all that?

We did many things through AIO, but all of my activities began to take their toll on my marriage. I knew a divorce was coming for several different reasons. First of all, Fred was stepping down from immense power and, as Miss Fixit, I should have gone into the void, filled it, and taken care of everything. Knowing that my husband was unhappy, my number one job was to make it right. But I got involved in AIO's projects. It was one of our peak times. We were organizing CERT [Council of Energy Resource Tribes], dealing with tribal resources, investigating environmental issues as a way of controlling development, having our own regulations, testing tribal boundaries and structures, putting seven federal agencies together on environmental issues, and many other projects. AIO went from one major project to another, and I was immersed in it. Fred was adjusting to an entirely different way of life at the same time, and I didn't pay enough attention to the marriage or how hard it was for Fred to make those adjustments.

During this time—it was right after Fred's losing primary campaign in 1976—we had a garage sale because we collectively decided that we wanted to move from Washington to New Mexico. My first choice was always New Mexico. In Oklahoma we would get entangled and embroiled in all the local politics. We looked at Colorado and Arizona, but both of them lacked some appeal. And, we were more familiar with New Mexico because we had traveled out here in the summer. We moved and stayed with my sister in Albuquerque for a while. We loved Corrales, and after an item appeared in the local newspaper about us, a realtor called and wondered if there was anything she could help us with.[1] She set up a whole bunch of houses for us to look at and during the second day of riding around we found a house in Corrales. It just moved really rapidly. Fred also got a job offer from the political science department at the University of New Mexico, so it all came together and seemed natural for us to live in New Mexico. I received permission from the AIO board to lead the organization from New Mexico, so we set up our offices in an Albuquerque bank building.

In 1980 I was asked by a group of citizens, including Barry Commoner—who was [and is still] a well-known environmentalist—to run for office. These folks thought that he would be a good candidate for president, and when they got together, they thought they would be very progressive and name a woman as his running mate on the Citizens' Party ticket.[2] One member of the group called me to see if I would be interested in being that candidate. When I agreed, they flew out to see me. At first I was concerned because I knew Fred was not happy, but Fred said, "Yes, you have to do it. If you don't, you'll always regret the fact that you didn't try." So, on Fred's recommendation, I said "yes," but still wanted to meet with Kathryn and Manuel in Washington to discuss the pros and cons. I thought they would be a little more objective. We put the pros and cons down on paper and decided that I would do it. But while Fred intellectually supported me, he found it very difficult for me to be gone at the time. [When I was chosen] I had a pretty good national reputation working with tribes and women's groups, so I think that's why I was selected. Also, I was a minority, so that helped.

My working relationship with [Barry Commoner] was really quite good. When we had strategy meetings, though I didn't feel quite good about them. So, I invited Kathryn and Margaret Gover to sit in with me and tell me what they thought was wrong with the discussions. During one of the breaks Kathryn said, "Mother, they are treating you like the candidate's wife." She was right, and then Margaret said, "You are acting like a candidate's wife." Of course! That was a role I was accustomed to and had a great comfort level in doing. One of the reasons that I wasn't an effective campaigner was that I was campaigning for Barry Commoner and not for myself, having never been in that particular position before. In the old days Fred and I campaigned together, and when I ran for the vice presidency I was out there by myself. He was teaching at the time and couldn't get off and never came and campaigned with me.

One of the planks in our platform was the creation of a safer environment, but we were really trying to start a third party. We believed that the two parties were so similar that you couldn't distinguish between both. We needed a forum to address corporate control of our economy and of our society. A prime example was what the corporations had done to our environment. At our Citizens' Party political convention in Cleveland, I was elected from the floor.

Being a candidate for vice president was probably one of the best and one of the worst things that ever happened to me. The pressures put on me were just terrible. It became so unpleasant that I found it more and more difficult to go out and campaign with any comfort level. I think the people in my life were afraid they were losing me. All of a sudden the whole experience of watching people around me from that perspective radically changed my behavior. I became liberated in the sense that I had to really act for myself and not depend on others to react to me. And that was good, but getting up and getting out to campaign put subconscious barriers up. In that regard it was a very terrible experience.

I remember flying to Hawaii during the campaign and being very well received. I was scheduled to stay with one family until I learned they had

cats. Because of my allergies I wound up staying in another house that looked like it came out of a Marlene Dietrich movie that I remember being called *Rain*. It had a tin roof. When the rain fell on it, I really felt like I was on a tropical island.

We didn't have a lot of money for the campaign so we routinely stayed in private houses. We got to know people who were ready for a third party all the way from Maine to Texas to Oregon and beyond. Meeting people and staying in their homes was one of the highlights of the campaign. I even stayed with a bishop in New York.

Even though we really didn't expect to win, we didn't withdraw. We campaigned all through the primaries. We really weren't running to get elected. We were running to start a third party, and we had to get on the ballot in a certain number of states. Talk about difficult! Every state has a different regulation and requirement to get on the ballot. Boy, it took ten times more energy to try to organize a third party than it does to run for an elective office. I don't know that we have true democracy in that sense because those barriers really keep a third voice from being heard and organized. I think the Libertarian Party has done that though, but I don't think they have gone anyplace with their organization.

The election results were terrible, as we imagined, but running for office did increase my national recognition. However, I don't know if it helped my efforts at running AIO. The year after that political campaign I got a divorce and moved AIO's offices to Washington.

Everything seemed to be going peachy keen in my marriage, but it wasn't, and I could tell. Somewhere I couldn't let go and stop my work and pay attention to my marriage. I was also very much involved in the women's movement and was helping to start the Women's Political Caucus. I was just moving into my own world. Still, when the end came, I was surprised—had to go to counseling. Fred went once. He said I was the one who was having problems, so he didn't have to continue. We knew how to avoid each other rather than have confrontations. He made the first move toward divorce and then I reacted. The whole thing wasn't very good for me because I had never been by myself, never in my life. It was horrifying. One piece of the counseling was that I had a sense of

abandonment that went all the way back to my father and mother. It was a hangover and was pretty hard for me.

Fortunately the children were all grown. Laura was in college with a room at the dorm. The other two kids had been gone for some time, and even though they were all terribly affected by it, they were very supportive. They all came to me and helped me select an attorney when we decided there wasn't any help for the relationship. The kids made sure of things for me, like getting to the attorney's office. They weren't necessarily afraid that Fred wouldn't treat me fairly, but they just wanted to make sure I was well represented. It was so hard for them, but another thing I learned in counseling was to get over it. However, I had to get back in touch with Fred in order to get my own feelings into some perspective so the children could do the same. I found it easier to work out my relationship with them than it was for them seeing us be comfortable together with the woman that Fred married shortly thereafter.

I still love him a great deal. He's been one of the most important figures in my life, and I want to keep that relationship. When we start talking we just fall right into talking about people and politics, like we used to do.

Oh, that was a hard year. I had been robbed of all my clothes in Washington while I was attending a birthday party given for me by Kathryn. Someone broke into my room in the small residential hotel where I was staying. The robbers had a bag and shoved all my clothes and jewelry into it and left me with a pair of panty hose and a jacket. That same year my brother-in-law died of cancer of the brain. His behavior before he died was so erratic, so terrible, so strange. He had been the only male figure in my life other than my grandfather and Fred. My sister didn't want to prolong his death but the doctor fought her on it. She made that horrible decision, and we all supported her. And I had a hysterectomy. Took it all in one blow. Then I got a divorce, and although I wanted it, there certainly was a big adjustment included.

Afterward, I went back to Washington as a single woman and lived there for ten years, working on AIO matters. Kathryn and Manuel were already there and found an apartment for me, a nice flat right down

on DuPont Circle, which was very attractive. Then they helped me get settled in. My secretary from New Mexico was also with me, as was my AIO administrator, who had been with me for ten years. They both were a tremendous help. I had gotten permission from the AIO board to leave New Mexico and move back to Washington, but the whole thing was very difficult. It was almost like taking a scraper, scraping everything clean, and starting all over again. The reason I moved back was to get away. It was just too emotional for me in New Mexico and I couldn't adjust to single life. Then too, Kathryn and Manuel were in Washington and Jimmy Carter's administration was just coming in. The year was 1977. Often I thought I was behaving so inappropriately, but there were no guidelines, no books for recently divorced women to read. I questioned my behavior, thought I was going crazy. Counseling didn't help too much. I talked with a couple of friends in New York, who told me things they did that were worse. I was really mediocre compared to them. That made me feel better, put things in perspective a little bit. But I hurt physically, went to a doctor, who said that's what [people] used to call "a heartbreak."

At first I was so angry, but mostly sad. I was so disappointed. First of all, I took all the blame, believing that if I had paid attention, I could have managed it all. Through the counseling I came to realize that I mainly felt sad. Then Fred got married. Gee. One of the silly things that angered me was that I had a box of stuff that I was convinced he wanted. He didn't, so I kept it. It's a joke between us now. He says, "I sure would like to have this or that, but it's in the box." Fred was very generous in the settlement and he made me a bet (which he never paid off) that I would be remarried in six months. The best thing that happened to me was having friends in Washington. We got a group of women together by accidentally running into each other at different social functions. Because holidays were so awful alone, we'd all get together and celebrate our birthdays and holidays. Needless to say, we were all divorced and networking. We are still close and they come out to New Mexico to see me. When I'm in Washington, I see them. Three of us went to Italy together last summer. We stay up with each other's

careers and children. When Laura got married, it was very difficult for me because she was the last of my children to leave the nest. I know that sounds trite, but it's the truth. My friends all acted as mothers of the bride, so she had four mothers in attendance. We all wore dresses of the same design, but different colors, including Mary Blackmon, who had lived with us and taken care of Laura. It was a fairy princess wedding in a big church on Sixteenth Street in Washington. Everyone there was very supportive of me. We decided to sing Comanche songs and all broke into tears. I never thought we'd finish, but we did, even though in the rehearsal we cried and cried and cried. Laura's wedding was wonderful.

Fred and his wife, Marg, were at the wedding also. I have such a good relationship with him now but had to kind of force it at first. Kathryn had gone into counseling over the divorce, and she urged me to go also, saying she didn't think I was quite adjusted over the whole thing. So I went with her to the Family Center at Georgetown University. I believe it was the first time a mother and daughter attended together. My counselor became a very good friend and gave me a number of insights that were valuable. For example, I learned how family systems have to overcome these difficulties and if you don't reconstitute yourself, the problems will always be hanging on your back. You'll have to be carrying negativity around with you all the time and filter everything through it. The counselor advised me to try to get some kind of relationship with Fred. I didn't have to because the kids were old enough to be on their own, but I chose to do it, forced it. Everybody was more uncomfortable than I was over the whole thing. We all spend part of Christmas Eve or Christmas day together. Maybe both. His new wife has been very tolerant, and even though the situation is unusual, it works. We are good friends. Fred and I have one grandchild, Laura's son Sam Fred. Fred and I usually call each other in regard to the children and what they are doing. Once in a while I call him about something or other, some little detail, or he'll call me. Just kind of an excuse to check on each other. So, we look out for each other. Still. And I think we will continue to do so. That's my hope.

My family is moving along perfectly, and I have great expectations that they will live up to their potential. They have strength and know-how. If we in the family work hard and keep them connected to their Comanche tribal values, I think they will continue to go far. And I hope the Comanche tribe will, in the future, become part of a global discussion, that people will come to see us and appreciate our different points of view and capture it in their political and social thinking. We Indians are past the colonialism physically, but we are not necessarily out of it politically. But I really do see a bright tomorrow for the young people.

For myself and for now, I want to sit out here [in New Mexico] and watch the sun go down. I'd like to start wearing Comanche dresses and let my hair grow long and do more meditation and thinking. I'd like to see if I can become some sort of a medicine woman as such. Through my medicine I'll be able to help people, not so much by making them well, but help them in their thinking and personal progress. Through meditation and thoughtfulness, I hope to call on those spirits that the old Comanches knew. "Communing with nature" has become kind of trite but I think there is a lot more for me to learn that way. I think I have played out all my human interrelations. As we Comanches believe, everyone has medicine and it is everyone's responsibility to help everyone else cultivate their strengths and medicine.

EPILOGUE:
A CONTINUING
MISSION

We want to change the whole federal system.

Those days seem so long ago, and yet I can't imagine where the time has gone. AIO has grown beyond my wildest dreams and today has a long list of accomplishments. The future, as I see it for AIO, should have two thrusts: to work on how tribal governments fit in with the federal systems and how to institutionalize tribes within the federal systems. The federal government really doesn't recognize us although they say they do. They don't know how to carry out a relationship with us because there's no structure in place to carry it out. Yes, they recognize tribes as government but only in one agency alone, the Environment Protection Agency (EPA), are tribes treated like tribal governments.[1] Generally, there is no clear perception that tribal governments are part of the political fabric of the country. It's not taught in school, we don't know anything about it, and therefore the decision makers and public policy people don't have that fact as part of their working knowledge. That's part of the reason we run up against attorneys general from time to time.

I want to create a standard and have been working on it from time to time, but it is just now coming into the minds of other folks. I think that among us we will figure out how to do it. By the time we educate one administration, though, a new one comes in and it's a whole new set of people who have no idea of what we're talking about.

We have to blame the educational institutions. Until now we Indians have been products of anthropologists who have determined who the Indian is and was. That's whom we depend upon even more than historians. Anthropologists have taken the initiatives, set the definition, knowledge, and acceptance of Indians from the museums to classes at the universities. Political scientists and policymakers have just, in this generation, acknowledged that tribes are governments, but it hasn't yet been part of the learning process within the general public. Every step we take we have to teach Indian 101, from an EPA Solid Waste employee to the White House to the attorney general to state legislators.

Indian people have to put up with this situation because we have not created a forum to deal with it. AIO was the first organization to articulate that as an issue. Within our own communities we have tried to fix the BIA in the past, but there was no recognition of the fact that there was no institution that allows tribal consideration before federal policies are applied, not afterwards. When we talk about states, counties, cities, and local governments, in most cases with just very few exceptions, tribal governments are as eligible for programs. Years ago I asked employees in both the Senate and the House how tribal governments could be considered eligible for funding along with local governments. It took these learned people, some with legal backgrounds, by surprise. They didn't even have the concept.

We Indians have dual citizenship. Not only are we citizens within our own tribes and are entitled to special resources under the treaties, but we are also entitled to everything any other citizen of the United States is entitled to. Because of that, the federal agencies opened up and that's how we got all those Indian desks in them and that's how Indian advisory groups appeared.

We're organized. We want to change the entire federal system. Changing the BIA doesn't amount to a hill of beans; we've done that. Every six to ten years we have reorganized the Bureau of Indian Affairs. The BIA is just part of a larger system of government. The bureau should just take care of the treaty trust responsibility. As governmental entities, Indian tribes should be as eligible as counties, cities, and states are for resources. After all, tribes have their own sovereign systems. Remember federalism? The federalist system allows that tribes are governmental entities, but in reality it really hasn't been applied. The government gives lip service to the idea. Tribes are governments and we have the right to govern, except for conducting international trade. Then we fall under the aegis of the United States. The BIA took over and treated us like colonial governments and controlled our lives. We have now thrown that yoke off, thanks to President Lyndon Johnson and the War on Poverty programs.

The whole 1960s movements also helped, as did AIM, who mouthed the word "sovereignty" first and scared the heck out of everybody else. AIO has taken the concept of sovereignty and used it as a base of operations to inform federal agencies about the status of tribes — as tribes see themselves in relation to the government. A lot of people, even those who talk about it, don't quite understand what sovereignty means. To me, it means the right to be self-governing over our own people and our own lands, and that we are a system of governments like the federal system. It doesn't mean that we are separate governments outside the United States system. We are part of the United States and therefore "sovereign" in that sense, like states are sovereign units within the federal system. Tribes are equal to the states but different than them in their relations to the federal government through treaties.

Bureaucrats have to pay attention to that and then agree because it won't work otherwise. But they are fighting it. Nonetheless, they have said "OK, it's national policy as stated by the Congress, by the mouth of the president, and by every federal agency." When they admit the tribes are on a government-to-government basis with the federal government, then we will say, "OK, here's how you deal with tribes on

that basis: you have to have an infrastructure. You cannot leave us out of the policymaking. We have to be part of it." In many ways, educating government personnel is a daunting task, but AIO is up to it. You can bet on that.

We have actually made some progress. Within a division of EPA, Solid Waste and Emergency Relief, we have now established a relationship equivalent to what the states have—a system that evaluates federal policies and determines whether they will be damaging to them as a unit of government. Our cooperative association has ensured that tribes will have the same access to government to be able to do the same. Tribes should be able to react to policy as it is being developed and then have a way of working with Congress on policies.

Through AIO's work in the past, EPA was the first agency to develop an Indian policy statement that acknowledges that they will deal with tribes on a government-to-government basis. We accomplished that by getting to know people and working with them within the agency. We created an environment that enabled the model relationship to function.

As a result, the Northern Cheyennes have now set their own environmental standards. That doesn't sound like a very big deal, but that's the process of carrying out sovereignty. It's a huge achievement, even though the Denver Regional Office of EPA fought it. Four major energy corporations wanted to strip mine the Cheyenne land, but the Cheyennes said it would be tantamount to cultural genocide because there would be thirty non-Indians to every Northern Cheyenne on the reservation to do the work. Their main concern was not economics, but was the fact that they might no longer exist as a people because the mining people would be disruptive to the culture. The Indians had for years been isolated up there on their land and it was through their knowledge of the Council of Energy Resource Tribes (CERT) and AIO that they came to us. We advised them to develop some regulations first of all and at the time were encouraging all tribes to develop regulations that protect their interests.

There's always a trade-off when you do any kind of development, even building houses. If you don't make the trade-off part of your

consideration in planning development, whether it be natural resources or housing, it will affect the outcome. Nobody paid attention to us or to what we were saying in those days but nowadays the biggest thing in the world is the environment. The Cheyennes used the environment as a weapon to stop development. They were the first governmental entity in the United States to set a high standard of air quality and it stopped on- and off-reservation development that could have impacted them adversely.

Their success was a major breakthrough in the mental attitude of the EPA. After that, with a staff person, we actually wrote the Indian policy statement used by the EPA. We also helped write the policies for the Departments of Energy and Agriculture. By that time we could wave our successes around. We learned that once a high official says "government-to-government" it doesn't necessarily dribble down to the worker bees in the agencies, so you have to show them how to implement the new concept. Yes, it's new for them but not for us Indians. It's an old concept of how to make the disconnect fit. For example, we got disconnected somewhere, and now we are trying to connect back up. This is our continuous mission. We do these little folksy things in order to implement the major mission. Nobody will fund us to do the major mission until it becomes acceptable to do so.

AMBASSADORS

In 1993 AIO launched a dynamic initiative to foster a new generation of Indian leaders within Native American communities. Based on traditional tribal values and wisdom, AIO's Ambassadors program takes some of the nation's brightest and most promising young Indian professionals through an intensive one-year program aimed at rekindling and reinforcing the use of their tribal values in a modern context. During the year, the participants interact with current and past leaders, explore their family and tribal histories, and learn to translate past experiences into positive solutions for the future. The Ambassadors program requires each participant to design and implement a community-based project that hones their leadership skills and is of direct benefit to their communities.

Each Ambassador is chosen by a committee of regional and national leaders, such as Michael Chapman (a Menominee), Wallace Coffey (a Comanche), Nedra Darling (a Potawatomi), Wilma Mankiller (a Cherokee), and Reuben Snake (a Winnebago). The diversity of the committee ensures that ambassadors come from many different backgrounds and bring the unique values of their tribe to the program.

LaDonna Harris and her wealth of experience and knowledge are at the heart of the program. Assisting her are two professors from the Native American Education Services (NAES) College, an Indian-run college in Chicago, with campuses on the Menominee and Ft. Peck Reservations. These professors— Dr. David Beck and Rosalyn LaPier—help develop the ambassadors' reading lists, design curricula, and facilitate discussions. They oversee the accreditation process of the Ambassadors through NAES College.

~

When I started the Ambassadors program, the leadership of most tribes was age sixty-five and older. Now leaders have become younger and younger. I don't know if that's good or bad. All of a sudden we have new leadership with no history as to how we Indians came to be as we are. The young people who go through our Ambassadors program must learn their tribal history and the work that AIO has done in several areas. It gives them a different view of issues and a couple of distinct advantages.

Getting the Ambassadors program funded by Kellogg in the amount of three million dollars was a major breakthrough in the mental attitude of foundations.[2] Usually these philanthropic sources fund little piddly bits of money, and, in some cases, substantial piddly bits of money, for three years and then they are gone, and Indian organizations are on their own; for example, the Bureau of Indian Affairs was through their programs by limiting itself to certain kinds of funding. That might work for some, for example the University of Oklahoma, because those groups can get state funding, but we Indians can't. In effect, the short funding periods contribute to our dysfunction. Where it used to be white folks in the bureau doing it to us, in some ways we do it to ourselves by continuing to apply for limited funding. We Indians then are not solving our own problems. The short-term money makes us responsible for both

the money and the program. In AIO we are not waiting for somebody to buy our ideas. We configure our Ambassadors program, for example, any way we want to; we are not trapped.

The non-gaming tribes could also learn philanthropy. One of the major foundations came to interview us at AIO and found out to their surprise that we were not "Lo! The poor Indian."[3] We didn't fit their stereotype. They only funded a continuation of the stereotype.

There is one tribe in South Dakota that will remain nameless. You can count every dollar that went in there and nothing has changed. But that's why the funding sources went into it. That way we can never get to the real pathology of the disease, and it keeps the poor Indian down so others can do good things for him. I call it the "missionary position." Funding sources love to say, "We are going to do good things to those people. Spread your legs and don't even kiss us." I try to be sensitive, but . . . in effect, well-meaning people became enablers and trapped us into dependency and dysfunction and pathology. Until we can interpret the pathology in a way to break us out of it, we will be trapped in these boxes forever.

Language contributes to our pathology as well. The terms that we Indians use for ourselves, such as "minorities" and "deprived," trap us in the state of mind of being victims. The historical and contemporary treatment of us Indians by the Bureau of Indian Affairs has made us reactionary instead of proactive people, so we get trapped in a reactive mode and don't know how to solve our own problems. We only know how to react when people do things to us. How can we get out of the pathology of being reactionary and into a proactive stance as open, thinking people? One of the ways is through funding. That's why AIO held a conclave of Indian leaders, our ambassadors, elected Indian officials, advisors, our board, poets—this year. Rather than have a class, we had a conclave through which many productive ideas emerged. We had fun too—music, songs, dances, all intermeshed with our thinking. There are not enough forums for Indians to conduct intellectual or philosophical thinking. What emerged from our meeting was a proactive way of looking at issues rather than lamenting that we are poor Indians whose treaties

were broken. That's why AIO developed the Tribal Issues Management Systems (TIMS), an issues-management and consensus-building process specifically for tribes.

AIO has always been proactive. Our structure permits it. We ask where something is leading, like CERT, for example. We asked questions at the time CERT was initiated and learned that there might be a global shortage of energy, of food, and if that was so, the Indians would be the first people impacted by that. Consequently, CERT was born to protect the energy resources that are on many reservations. Why are we the poorest people in the country when we own land? When we own the resources? Nobody could tell us how much or how many resources we owned. It's asking those kinds of questions that places AIO on the cutting edge. After we Indians started controlling our resources, we created an environment where new leadership could come forward and take it over. After CERT was organized, the fish tribes organized, the timber tribes organized, and the agricultural tribes organized.

Controlling resources means having your own regulations. AIO did it, and it was an evolutionary thought process for us. We moved to a new position of thinking, and we could then let go. It's one of those hard things to do because we all are taught through a Euro-American system that when you create something, you never let it go. We learned that fact during our first two years in organizing AIO. Let go. You leave something in place for others. In Indian values you shouldn't own anything you can't give away, whether it's ideas or anything. You ought to be able to give it away. It frees you up, too. It's basic Indian philosophy and wisdom. Our ancestors knew that ownership was burdensome and selfish. The more ownership you have, the more selfish you get, the more power you have to have, and the more control you have to have.

Knowing this is how one comes to have greater appreciation for cultural values. There is a renewed need for the innate wisdom that created these values. The ancestors were real psychologists who understood human qualities so much better than all the European mental health experts at the time. The whole Indian social-political structure allows individual freedom. If you don't trample on somebody else, you are so

much freer. So, if you see it as a gift, as being able to do things in the Indian way, you don't get all uptight about it.

Charlie Loha, a crazy Osage on AIO's board, said, "Well, we have created a lot of Frankensteins, too." That's absolutely true. We have created as many things by accident as we have by planning, but we have been flexible enough to see it. What Kellogg has done by giving AIO this money has broken traditional philanthropy gift giving, particularly to Indians. This is Kellogg's great experiment. We have to look at it that way and foster it in a way that is different from everything else we have ever done.[4]

With the funding, we will break ground by showing potential resources how native groups can be innovators. We at AIO like to think we are somewhat smart. Something always elevates us to a new level of consciousness. No, we don't want to say we know all the answers. Any real Indian will say that an individual doesn't know the answers. What works for me works for me, but we can help you get to another level of consciousness, not just from what we say but from what you know and what you have been exposed to. It helps you move to another place. I like to use that term. I always hope to be able to move to another place. I'd like to get back home to see if I could be like the old Comanche people and think in a different way. It makes me think of my grandmother.

NOTES

PREFACE

1. The epigraphs that open each chapter have been taken from the transcribed interviews with LaDonna Harris.

2. LaDonna Harris and Jacqueline Wasilewski, *This Is What We Want to Share: Core Cultural Values* (Bernalillo NM: Americans for Indian Opportunity, 1992), p. 7.

3. Harris, *This is What We Want to Share*, p. 48

4. Harris, *This is What We Want to Share*, pp. 36–40.

1. WHERE I CAME FROM

1. Walters is the county seat of Cotton County. The post office was established on 27 September 1901. Until 23 July 1917, the official name was Walter, named for William R. Walter, a prominent local resident. George Shirk, *Oklahoma Place Names* (Norman: University of Oklahoma Press, 1974), p. 249.

2. D. S. Otis, *The Dawes Act and the Allotment of Indian Lands* (Norman: University of Oklahoma Press, 1973), pp. 6–7. Another excellent discussion of the Dawes Act and its history and consequences is contained in Loring Benson

Priest, *Uncle Sam's Stepchildren: The Reformation of United States Indian Policy, 1865–1887* (New York: Octagon Books, 1972). In particular, Priest reviews the defects in the early attempts at designing severalty legislation (pp. 178–87), the debates of the 1880s (pp. 188–97), the controversy over Indian citizenship (pp. 198–216), the development of Indian land policies (pp. 217–32), and the Dawes Act and Indian reform (pp. 248–52). Additional sources of information include Leonard A. Carlson, *Indians, Bureaucrats, and Land: The Dawes Act and the Decline of Indian Farming* (Westport CT: Greenwood, 1981), and Wilcomb E. Washburn, *The Assault on Indian Tribalism: The General Allotment Law (Dawes Act) of 1887* (Philadelphia: J. B. Lippincott, 1975).

One of the main objections to the Dawes Act by congressmen sympathetic to the natives was that the legislation was not designed to help the Indians as much as to provide a method for getting at the valuable Indian lands and opening them up to white settlement. Assimilation was the recognized goal of national Indian policy, and allotment came to be seen as the proper means of achieving that goal.

3. Lawton is the county seat of Comanche County. The post office was established on 15 July 1901; the town was named for Maj. Gen. Henry W. Lawton, killed during the Philippine Insurrection. Shirk, *Oklahoma Place Names*, p. 138. According to author Dan Thrapp, Lawton was responsible for directing the slaughter of more than one thousand Comanche ponies captured at Palo Duro Canyon, Texas, in 1874. LaDonna Harris's ancestors were in the canyon at the time. Dan L. Thrapp, *Encyclopedia of Frontier Biography*, 3 vols. (Lincoln: University of Nebraska Press, with the Arthur H. Clark Company, Spokane WA, 1988), 2:821.

4. The role of family in Comanche life has always been extremely important. Historically, the bands such as Quahada and Yamparika were actually family groups in the main, and were fairly autonomous units. Grandfather John Tabbytite was Yamparika and Grandmother Wick-kie Tabbytite was Quahada. LaDonna Harris considers herself to be a member of the Quahada band and, when asked, identifies herself as such.

5. Quanah Parker was born to a white mother and Quahada Comanche chief Peta Nocona in 1845. As a noted raider, he was prominent in the battle of Adobe Walls and surrendered at Fort Sill after the Palo Duro event. He

became the Comanches' principal spokesman and accepted a reservation for his tribe in southwestern Oklahoma around 1875. For the next thirty years he was committed to the ways of peace for his people. He encouraged education and agriculture and became an astute businessman among members of the surrounding communities. He died near Fort Sill on 23 February 1911 and is buried in the post cemetery near his mother. Thrapp, *Encyclopedia of Frontier Biography*, 3:1113. Literature about Quanah Parker abounds, and includes Bill Neeley, *The Last Comanche Chief: The Life and Times of Quanah Parker* (New York: J. Wiley, 1995), and William T. Hagan, *Quanah Parker: Comanche Chief* (Norman: University of Oklahoma Press, 1993).

6. Ernest Wallace and E. Adamson Hoebel, *The Comanches: Lords of the Southern Plains* (Norman: University of Oklahoma Press, 1952), pp. 193–93, relates two Comanche creation myths that are different from each other; neither contains any reference to little people with bows and arrows. It is not unusual for a society to have several creation myths that are dissimilar or contain variations of the same story.

7. Ten Bears spoke for the Comanches at the Council of Medicine Lodge Creek in 1867. Wallace and Hoebel, *The Comanches*, p. 282, calls his speech "a masterpiece of oratory."

8. Wallace and Hoebel, *The Comanches*, p. 66.

9. Researcher Col. W. S. Nye believes that thirteen to fifteen Indian warriors were killed (*Carbine and Lance: The Story of Old Fort Sill* [Norman: The University of Oklahoma Press, 1988], p. 191), but Ms. Harris's statement implies that many more were dead.

10. For more information on the battle of Palo Duro Canyon, see Wallace and Hoebel, *The Comanches*, pp. 325–27, and Nye, *Carbine and Lance*, pp. 221–25.

11. Nye, *Carbine and Lance*, p. 261.

12. Nye, *Carbine and Lance*, pp. 261–62. In 1897 the War Department disbanded all the Indian troops.

13. This reference is to M.Sgt. Morris Swett, a librarian at Fort Sill who, in his forty years on the job, preserved voluminous material including correspondence, records, and photos that might otherwise have been lost. Swett wrote a brief but most informative history of Fort Sill that was part of a compilation produced by the Lawton Business and Professional Woman's Club. Called *'Neath the*

August Sun—1901, it was published by N. T. Plummer Printing in Anadarko, Oklahoma, in 1933. Swett's article begins on page 26.

14. Burnett (1 Jan. 1849–26 June 1922) and his family settled in Denton County, Texas, in 1856, having migrated from Bates County, Missouri. He became an early trail driver, trail boss, and then his father's partner. In 1870 he acquired the famous 6666 brand in Wichita County, Texas, and started his own herd. Legend has it that he won the ranch in a poker game with four sixes, but his family has denied the story. He is credited with starting the idea of all-steer beef herds; in 1875 he introduced blooded Durhams and Herefords onto his ranch. As a friend of Quanah Parker, Burnett leased acreage from the Comanches for grazing his stock. For more information, see Thrapp, *Encyclopedia of Frontier Biography*, 1:195.

15. This is a reference to grass money, an important concept. Foster reported, "Beginning in 1885, Comanches entered into lease arrangements with Texas ranchers for reservation pastures. The arrangement lasted until 1906 and provided each Comanche with a semiannual 'grass' payment. The payment of grass money probably went a long way toward securing Comanche subsistence for the remainder of the reservation period." Morris W. Foster, *Being Comanche: A Social History of an American Indian Community* (Tucson: University of Arizona Press, 1991), p. 81.

16. The house was probably built as a "thank-you" to Quanah from the ranchers who leased Comanche lands. A photo of the house with Quanah Parker standing on the balcony is in David La Vere, *Life among the Texas Indians: The WPA Narratives* (College Station: Texas A & M University Press, 1998), p. 117.

2. A COMANCHE GIRLHOOD

1. Wallace and Hoebel, *The Comanches*, p. 32.

2. James Mooney, "The Aboriginal Population of America North of Mexico," *Smithsonian Miscellaneous Collections* 80, no. 7 (1928): 13.

3. When Fred Harris was a U.S. senator, he and LaDonna took her grandmother to Washington DC. "She just took over the town," reported Fred. She went to the White House and met President and Mrs. Johnson and spoke with a reporter from the *Washington Post* who asked her what in Washington

impressed her the most. "The plants," said Mrs. Tabbytite. "That's what I liked the most." Fred noted, "Anytime we went somewhere in Washington, for example to George Washington's home, she'd take a little piece of a plant. Then she'd put a little water on a Kleenex to protect the plant. When she got home, she planted it, and it grew. Everywhere she went, she got plants. She really did have a green thumb." Fred R. Harris, interview with author, Albuquerque NM, 8 October 1997.

4. For an excellent study of the Indian boarding school systems, see David Wallace Adams, *Education for Extinction: American Indians and the Boarding School Experience, 1875–1928* (Lawrence: University Press of Kansas, 1995).

5. Formerly Botsford, Temple is located in Cotton County, eight miles southeast of Walters. The post office name was changed to Temple on 8 August 1902, named for Temple Houston, son of Texas's Sam Houston. Shirk, *Oklahoma Place Names*, p. 233.

6. LaDonna reckons time differently than many others. For Comanches, as for many native peoples, everything is relative, and so dates and times are often "fuzzy."

7. An off-reservation Indian boarding school that opened in 1884 in Lawrence, Kansas.

8. Located in Oklahoma County, adjoining Oklahoma City on the west. The post office was established on 11 March 1913. Its name comes from the Biblical community adjoining the city of Jerusalem. Shirk, *Oklahoma Place Names*, p. 23. Perhaps Bethany's most noted native son is Gary S. Hart, former Democratic senator and presidential aspirant.

9. The town takes its name from nearby Cache Creek, a tributary of the Red River. The name is French and means an underground storage pit.

10. A good discussion of traditional Comanche religion is in chapter 7 of Wallace and Hoebel, *The Comanches*. The traditional and modern roles of peyote in Comanche life are addressed extensively in Foster, *Being Comanche*.

11. A county in southwestern Oklahoma, organized on 28 August 1912 from the southern portion of Comanche County. Officially proclaimed on 18 November 1912 by Governor Lee Cruce, it took its name from the county's principal agricultural product. Walters is its county seat. Shirk, *Oklahoma Place Names*, p. 60.

12. Along with no prohibitions against more than one wife, Comanches observed several forms of affinal marriage. Wallace and Hoebel, *The Comanches*, p. 138, reports that the "levirate and sororate were the strongest of these. The number of wives might run anywhere from one to six or more. It was a normal pattern for a man to take as wives the younger sister or sisters of his first wife and any women he might have captured or girls who grew up as captives in the tribe." LaDonna said the practice of polygamy ceased when the Christians came along and that her grandfather "followed the law." LaDonna Harris, interview with author, Bernalillo NM, 3 January 1997.

13. The concept and meaning of "community" to Comanches is discussed extensively in Foster, *Being Comanche*. Identification as a Comanche is maintained in the eyes of the community by individuals returning every so often to participate in rituals of Comanche life. In so doing, the person who has left reaffirms his traditional and important relationships with his family and with the group as a whole.

14. Three other men in LaDonna Harris's family were also killed in motor vehicle accidents. Her Uncle Clinton was driving a truck on an icy bridge and was sober when the tragedy occurred. Frank Jr. was killed at a different time. Larry, who didn't drink, went out with some friends who were drinking and was killed at the foot of Mt. Scott near Lawton.

3. LEARNING, LOVING, AND LIVING

1. LaDonna's words of caution about law enforcement personnel have not been lost on her children. The eldest, Kathryn, majored in social relations in college, with a concentration in prison systems. "I had been raised being afraid of police," she told me in October 1997. "I had wanted to study them because anything that has power over me, I want to understand it and get a grasp on it, particularly the abuse of power."

2. N. Scott Momaday (1934–), a Kiowa Indian, was born in Lawton but grew up on the Navajo Reservation. He earned his M.A. and Ph.D. degrees from Stanford University in 1960 and 1963, respectively. He has garnered critical acclaim for his focus on Kiowa traditions, customs, and beliefs, and is also recognized as one of the most successful contemporary Native American literary

figures. Two of his best-known books are *A House Made of Dawn* (1968) and *The Way to Rainy Mountain* (1969). At least two biographies about Momaday have been published: Adkins and Adkins, *N. Scott Momaday* (New York: McMillan, 1998) and Matthias Schubnell, *N. Scott Momaday: The Cultural and Literary Background* (Norman: University of Oklahoma Press, 1986). Also available is Charles L. Woodard, *Ancestral Voice: Conversations with N. Scott Momaday* (Lincoln: University of Nebraska Press, 1989).

3. Kathryn Harris Tijerina is today a special assistant to the chief justice of the New Mexico Supreme Court. She attended the University of Oklahoma from 1967 to 1969, then transferred to Radcliffe, where she graduated Magna Cum Laude in 1972. In 1975 she received a J.D. from Stanford University Law School. Her work history is equally impressive. During the years 1975–76 she conducted legal research in all areas of Indian law for the American Indian Policy Review Commission, which was a joint committee of Congress. The next year she was Senator James Abourezk's legislative assistant and from there became counsel to the U.S. Senate Committee on Indian Affairs. From 1978 to 1982 she was an Indian affairs specialist for the U.S. Department of Energy and then moved to New Mexico where from 1982 to 1984 she was the director of the Indian Resource Development (IRD) at New Mexico State University in Las Cruces. From 1984 to 1987 she enjoyed a governor's appointment as the deputy secretary of the state Natural Resource Department and then went back to the IRD for two years. From 1989 to 1993 Kathryn was president of the Institute of American Indian Arts in Santa Fe, New Mexico, and then became the director of Cultural and Recreational Services for the city of Albuquerque, New Mexico. She has been married to Manuel Tijerina, a law school classmate, since about a year after graduation. LaDonna is very proud of her.

4. In 1974 there were nine Indians at Stanford Law School, according to Kathryn Harris Tijerina. In an interview in October 1997 she told me, "These were not necessarily people who were enrolled members of tribes either. They were just people who self-identified as Indians." Although it seems the number of Indian students in law schools did not increase very much between the time father and daughter were law students, the situation appears to have now changed.

4. POLITICS AND PARTNERSHIP

1. Foster states that prior to allotment there were only a few Comanche Christians on the list of converts at the Deyo Baptist Mission. After allotment, however, the number increased dramatically. For example, between 1892 and 1901 (before allotment), there were only 13 Comanche converts, but between 1902 and 1911 (after allotment), there were 150 at the Deyo Mission. "Within a decade of allotment, at least six churches with Comanche membership were attracting converts." Foster, *Being Comanche*, p. 120.

2. In 1918 Mabel Dodge Lujan, a wealthy heiress from Buffalo, New York, went to Taos, New Mexico, met and married a Taos Pueblo Indian named Tony Lujan, and built a home on the outer edge of pueblo land. Celebrated artists, writers, and thinkers of the day flocked to their home, and some later stayed in northern New Mexico, including D. H. Lawrence, Andrew Dasburg, Georgia O'Keefe, Leon Gaspard, Ansel Adams, Mary Austin, Robinson Jeffers, Laura Gilpin, and Jean Toomer.

3. Foster, *Being Comanche*, p. 137.

4. Byron had a Comanche naming ceremony conducted by an old man who was a very good friend of LaDonna's grandmother. Comanches once didn't give names of the deceased to others, but that now seems to have changed. According to LaDonna, "An elder, who is dead now, said it was a good thing to remember those people. We should honor their names and carry them on because they were great warriors. It used to be that we had to be very careful with that and that's how I grew up. But Byron received my great-grandfather's name [and Don Baldwin's] and my grandson Sam Fred has his great-great-grandfather's name, the one who participated in the battle of Adobe Walls, so now we have both in the family. Papa wouldn't go to Byron's naming ceremony and said to me in Comanche, 'I know your grandmother thinks so much of this old man and he is nice now, but we don't know about his past. He could have done some wicked things.' If that person is wicked, [the trait] could be transferred to the person [who carries his name]. Papa refused to participate, but at the last minute, he came out and helped. Now when Byron acts up we say 'Papa was right.' Byron is now a member of the Comanche's Little Pony Society, a group that does charitable work in collecting food. It's nice that they are trying to be more proactive in the community and don't just put on the

Comanche dances." LaDonna Harris, interview with author, Bernalillo NM, 23 January 1997.

5. Still quite active in addressing a broad range of socioeconomic problems in innovative ways, Oklahomans for Indian Opportunity is a Native American charitable and educational nonprofit organization with a thirty-year history. OIO's overall purpose is to improve the social, cultural, and economic opportunities and conditions of American Indians and Alaskan Natives by facilitating their active participation in the state and national economy and culture while perpetuating the history and heritage of native peoples. The early programs of OIO were developed with Oklahoma tribes and native organizations. Their efforts included tribal council training, leadership training, youth development, work orientation, strategic planning, job development, entrepreneurship training, community economic development projects, food co-ops, and urban outreach centers. OIO's web site can be accessed at *http://www.telepath.com/oio*.

6. The Comanche tribe today honors each student individually, whether he or she graduates from college, high school, a trade school, or any other educational facility. The tribe holds a banquet, and the student gets a certificate from the school. Importantly, it is a public recognition by the tribe and the community of the individual's achievement. LaDonna believes that the Comanches now have the highest level of individuals who graduate from high school and college.

7. The Office of Economic Opportunity regulations prohibited off-reservation Indian groups from being awarded funding.

8. Beginning in 1885 Comanches entered into lease arrangements with Texas cattlemen for grazing rights on their pastures. The payment was known as grass money. Foster, *Being Comanche*, p. 81.

9. An historically peaceful tribe, the Choctaws were forced to cede their lands in Mississippi and Alabama and to move to Oklahoma where they established their own government, modeled after the U.S. government. It endured until the twentieth century, when it and the similar political organizations of the other four so-called civilized tribes, the Cherokees, Chickasaws, Creeks, and Seminoles, were absorbed by the State of Oklahoma. John Upton Terrell, *American Indian Almanac* (New York: Thoman Y. Crowell, 1974), p. 149. For more information about the Choctaws, see Clara Sue Kidwell, *Choctaws and Missionaries in Mississippi, 1818–1918* (Norman: University of Oklahoma Press,

1995), and Patritia Galloway, *Choctaw Genesis: 1500–1700* (Lincoln: University of Nebraska Press, 1998).

10. Morris Foster believed that in 1943 Congress attempted to end its treaty obligations to Native Americans by abolishing the Bureau of Indian Affairs. It wasn't until 1961 and the end of the Eisenhower administration, according to Foster, that the threat receded and the BIA remained. Foster, *Being Comanche*, p. 136. For more information about termination, see Donald Fixico, *Termination and Relocation: Federal Indian Policy, 1945–1960* (Albuquerque: University of New Mexico Press, 1986).

11. The Menominee tribe lived in the area known as Wisconsin for thousands of years. In 1954 Congress enacted the Termination Act, taking away Menominee recognition as Indians and dissolving U.S. trust responsibility. The tribe then no longer existed in the eyes of the United States and became subject to the State of Wisconsin taxation laws and regulations. For more information on the Menominees, see Leonard Bloomfield, *Menomini Texts* (AMS, 1990).

12. Ada Deer was born on the Menominee reservation in 1935. She was the first member of her tribe to graduate from the University of Wisconsin in Madison and the first American Indian to receive a master's degree from the School of Social Work at Columbia University in New York. In the early 1970s she helped her tribe overturn its termination. She built coalitions, lobbied members of the House and Senate, and rallied supporters around the country. On 22 December 1973, President Richard Nixon signed the Menominee Restoration Act, which was the first time Congress reversed itself in a specific matter of Indian policy. She then became the tribal chair. She was nominated by President Bill Clinton on 11 May 1993, to become assistant secretary for Indian affairs [also known as the head of the BIA] and was confirmed by the U.S. Senate on 16 July 1993. She was the first woman to hold that position in the history of the Department of the Interior. A more complete biography of Ada Deer can be found in Gretchen M. Bataille, ed., *Native American Women: A Biographical Dictionary* (New York: Garland, 1993), pp. 76–78.

5. IN THE CAPITAL

1. At thirty-three years of age, James Howard Edmonson was elected in 1958 as Oklahoma's youngest governor. A member of a politically conscious family

from Muskogee, Edmonson had won local fame for battling corruption in local and county government. As the state's chief executive, he continued this battle at the state level.

2. Oil man Robert S. Kerr first held elective office when he became Oklahoma's governor in 1942. During the war years he presided over a vigorous economic expansion and directed a remarkably efficient administration. A year after leaving the governor's office he was successful in his first attempt at the U.S. Senate in 1948. Kerr was reelected to two more terms. After he failed at winning the 1952 Democratic presidential nomination, Kerr devoted his energies to building his Senate career. Kerr served on several key committees, most notably the Finance and Public Works committees. For more information, see Anne Morgan, *Robert S. Kerr: The Senate Years* (Norman: University of Oklahoma Press, 1980).

3. A. S. (Almer Stilwell) "Mike" Monroney served thirty years in the U.S. Congress, first as the representative of the Fifth District of Oklahoma (1939–51) and later as a U.S. senator (1951–69). A moderate liberal in the House, he supported most of the New Deal and Fair Deal legislation but swayed from the party line on many labor issues. Monroney received his greatest accolades in his efforts to reorganize government; he cosponsored resolutions to create the Joint Committee on the Organization of Congress. While in the House he served on the Banking and Currency Committee and worked for price and rent controls.

4. Walter F. Mondale was the forty-second vice president of the United States, in office from 20 January 1977 to 20 January 1981, while Jimmy Carter was president. Prior to 1977 Mondale had been a U.S. senator (D-Minn). In 1984 he was defeated by Ronald Reagan in his bid to become president.

5. HEW is now the Department of Health and Human Services (DHHS).

6. From 1947 to 1977 Carl Albert served as the representative to the U.S. House of Representatives from Oklahoma's third district. During the last three terms, he was the Speaker of the House. Known as the "Little Giant from Little Dixie," Albert held more power than any other Oklahoman. For more information, see Carl Albert and Danney Goble, *Little Giant: The Life and Times of Speaker Carl Albert* (Norman: University of Oklahoma Press, 1990).

6. WASHINGTON DC INSIDERS

1. The Kerner Commission was assembled on 27 July 1967, following racial tension and riots. Chaired by Governor Otto Kerner of Illinois, the commission had many responsibilities, including studying the 1967 riots, looking into whether each riot followed a distinct pattern, investigating whether there was planning or organization in the riots, addressing the causes of the riots, tracing the history of black protests, examining the reasons why ghettos persisted, discussing the problems of unemployment, family structure, and social disorganization in the ghettos, and comparing the experiences of immigrants and blacks. The Kerner Commission found an "explosive mixture" in American cities, fed by pervasive discrimination and segregation in employment, education, and housing; black in-migration and white exodus, which had provided a growing crisis of deteriorating facilities and services and unmet human needs; the black ghettos, where segregation and poverty converged on the young to destroy opportunity and enforce failure. The Kerner Commission found eleven "deeply held grievances" in the communities it studied. In descending order of intensity, those grievances were: police practices, unemployment and underemployment, inadequate housing, poor recreation facilities and programs, ineffectiveness of the political structure and grievance mechanisms, disrespectful white attitudes, discriminatory administration of justice, inadequacy of federal programs, inadequacy of municipal services, discriminatory consumer and credit practices, and inadequate welfare programs.

The Kerner Commission conducted perhaps the most comprehensive study ever of lack of opportunity and economic inequality in American cities. The commission also offered a comprehensive approach to ameliorate most of the problems it identified: (1) to increase employment, the commission recommended that the federal government create two million new jobs and support job training programs through direct subsidies and tax incentives; (2) to promote educational opportunity, it recommended sharply increasing efforts to eliminate de facto segregation, extending early childhood education to every disadvantaged child in the country, and providing substantial federal funding for compensatory education programs at schools serving disadvantaged children; (3) to reform the welfare system, which it found "provides assistance well below the minimum necessary for a decent level of existence and imposes restrictions

that encourage continued dependency," the commission recommended a broad system of income supplementation that "would involve substantially greater federal expenditures than anything now contemplated"; and (4) to increase the availability of decent housing, the commission recommended expanding the rent supplement program, creating comparable ownership programs to make home ownership possible for low-income families, and expanding federal public housing programs, with a particular emphasis on placing low- and moderate-income housing outside of ghetto areas.

One major conclusion reached by members of the Kerner Commission warned that our nation was moving toward two societies, one black, one white—separate and unequal. The final report called for social programs on an unprecedented scale to correct the problem, giving renewed momentum to the Great Society initiatives of President Johnson.

For more information on the Kerner Commission, see Barbara Ritchie, ed., *The Riot Report—A Shortened Version of the Report of the National Advisory Commission on Civil Disorders* (New York: Viking, 1969).

2. Kathryn Harris Tijerina, interview with author, Albuquerque NM, 6 October 1997.

3. In the foreword to William H. Grier and Price M. Cobbs, *Black Rage* (New York: Bantam, 1968), Fred Harris wrote, "This book is crucially important. I can only hope its message is heeded. That message is simple, that despite the passage of five civil rights bills since 1957, despite the erosion of legal supports for segregated institutions, it is still no easy thing to be a black person in America. Without question the hour is late and the message of this book is grim. But the restoration of domestic tranquility to this land depends on our understanding and heeding it."

4. The Taos Indians, living in Taos, New Mexico, had been fighting for sixty years to regain their sacred tribal lands. For decades tribal leaders contended with unenlightened or frankly acquisitive incursions on their land by private exploiters and political administration representatives. This battle became the focus of a national debate and the centerpiece for an entirely new governmental approach to Indian affairs. Taos Blue Lake is considered by the Taos Indians to be a sacred life source and final resting place for their souls.

For a detailed description of the situation, see also Michael Lieder and Jake Page, *Wild Justice: The People of Geronimo vs. the United States* (New York: Random House, 1997), pp. 192–94. The authors call the lake "the central symbol of the [Taos] Indians' religion as the cross is in Christianity." A brief history of the property follows and concludes with, "Finally, in December 1970, Congress, led by the unlikely alliance of President Richard Nixon (one of the most sympathetic White House occupants that Indians have ever had) and two liberal senators, Edward Kennedy and Fred Harris, adopted legislation returning the entire area to the Indians." The legislation became P.L. No. 91-550, 84 Stat. 1437 (1970).

5. This dispute, like so many others in Indian country, involves treaty rights to the land and mineral resources. In a nutshell, the question is, "Who owns the land? Is it the government of the United States or the Indian people?"

6. For more information on the federal policy of Indian termination, see Fixico, *Termination and Relocation*; Kenneth R. Philip, *Indian Self-Rule: First-Hand Accounts of Indian-White Relations from Roosevelt to Reagan* (Logan: Utah State University Press, 1995); and Kenneth R. Philip, *Termination Revisited: American Indians on the Trail to Self-Determination, 1933–1953* (Lincoln: University of Nebraska Press, 1999).

7. Financed largely by philanthropic foundations, corporations, and private individuals, the Brookings Institution is world renowned for its unique ability to bridge the gap between scholarship and application and to carry out research and educational activities.

8. Relocation was another technique that the government thought would result in assimilation. Certain Indian adults were literally taken off their reservations and relocated in urban areas where they were expected to work and eventually "fit in" with the dominant culture all around them. It didn't work.

9. Laura Harris, interview with author, Bernalillo NM, 15 October 1997.

10. The American Indian Movement (AIM) has been one of the major Indian movements in the latter part of the twentieth century. Members were heavily involved in the occupation of Alcatraz in 1969 and the Wounded Knee conflict in 1973. For more information on AIM see Ward Churchill and James Vanderwall, *Agents of Repression: The FBI's Secret Wars against the Black Panther Party and The American Indian Movement* (Boston: South End, 1988); Paul Chaat Smith and

Robert Allen Warrior, *Like a Hurricane: The Indian Movement from Alcatraz to Wounded Knee* (New York: New Press, 1996); and Kenneth S. Stern, *Loud Hawk: The United States Versus the American Indian Movement* (Norman, University of Oklahoma Press, 1994).

11. Vine DeLoria Jr. is a member of a distinguished family of American Indians, with scholars, clergymen, and warrior chiefs as ancestors. He is an attorney and a professor of history, law, religious studies, and political science at the University of Colorado in Boulder.

12. The National Congress of American Indians was founded in 1944 and is the oldest, largest, and most representative national Indian organization serving the needs of a broad membership of American Indian and Alaska Native governments. The founding members stressed the need for unity and cooperation among tribal governments and people for the security and protection of treaty and sovereign rights. As a preeminent national Indian organization, NCAI is organized as a representative congress aiming for consensus on national priority issues.

13. Founded by LaDonna Harris in 1970, Americans for Indian Opportunity (AIO) was "created to serve as a catalyst for new concepts and opportunities for Indian people and is devoted to issues relating to tribal leadership and governance. AIO creates coalitions among tribes and between Indians and non-Indians to enhance the cultural, social, political, and economic self-sufficiency of tribes. AIO also builds on the foundation of traditional tribal wisdom and creates new pathways to incorporate those values in a modern context." (Undated press release).

7. ACTIVISM

1. The Shinnecocks are a Long Island, New York, subtribe of the Metoacs, and are located in Suffolk County. They speak the Algonquin language with a dialect similar to that of tribes in eastern Connecticut and Rhode Island. In 1600 the population of all the Metoac tribes was probably somewhere around 10,000, but the combined effects of warfare and epidemics during the next sixty years were devastating. By 1659 less than 500 Metoacs remained on Long Island. By 1788 their numbers had fallen to 162, and the 1910 census listed 167 Shinnecocks, 29 Montauks, and one Poosepatuck. Currently, there are two reservations on

Long Island: the Shinnecock, with nearly 400 residents, and the Poosepatuck Reserve, with 200 Unkechaug. Besides those on the reservations there are more than 1400 Metoacs living in the immediate area. Although the state of New York attempted to close the reservations during the 1930s, state recognition of the Shinnecocks and Unkechaugs dates from the colonial period. However, since they have not signed treaties with the United States, neither tribe is federally recognized.

2. The name Ojibwe (which also refers to Chippewa, though most now prefer to be called Anishinaabe) means "to roast until puckered up." It refers not to food but to a peculiar type of moccasin they made which had a "puckered" seam. In prehistoric times the Ojibwes were probably the largest individual tribe north of Mexico. In early historic times they occupied an enormous territory, from Sault Ste. Marie on the east, through the Upper Peninsula of Michigan, across northern Minnesota and southern Manitoba, and as far west as the Turtle Mountains of North Dakota. Terrell, *American Indian Almanac*, p. 244. For more information on the Ojibwes, see Melissa Meyer, *The White Earth Tragedy: Ethnicity and Dispossession at a Minnesota Anishinaabe Reservation, 1889–1920* (Lincoln: University of Nebraska Press, 1994); Gerald Vizenor, ed., *Summer in the Spring: Anishinaabe Poems and Stories* (Norman, University of Oklahoma Press, 1993); Ronald N. Satz, et al., *Chippewa Treaty Rights: The Reserved Rights of Wisconsin's Chippewa Indians in Historical Perspective* (Madison: University of Wisconsin Press, 1997); Edmund Jefferson Danziger, *The Chippewas of Lake Superior* (Norman, University of Oklahoma Press, 1990); Basil Johnston, illus. David Beyer, *Ojibway Heritage* (Lincoln: University of Nebraska Press, 1990); and M. Inez Hilger and Kimberly M. Blaeser, *Chippewa Families: A Social Study of White Earth Reservation, 1938* (Lincoln: University of Nebraska Press, 1990).

8. SPREADING WINGS

1. Corrales is a rural village about fifteen to twenty miles upriver from Albuquerque. Originally a Spanish settlement, the town is now struggling to retain its character and traditional ways.

2. Barry Commoner (1917–) joined the faculty of Washington University in St. Louis in 1947. In his thirty-four years there he explored viral function and led cellular research with implications for cancer diagnosis. Alarmed in

the early 1950s by the health risks posed by atomic testing, Commoner helped found the St. Louis Committee for Nuclear Information. In 1966 he established the Center for the Biology of Natural Systems to study human relationship with the environment. The author of many books and the 1980 Citizens' Party presidential candidate, he was a pioneer in the creation of the environmental movement and was termed the Paul Revere of Ecology. In May 1997 a program entitled "Barry Commoner's Contribution to the Environmental Movement: Science and Social Action," held in Cooper Union, New York, attracted speakers from around the world. Commoner's books include a 1992 publication, *Making Peace with the Planet*, in which he states, "The issue we face . . . is not how to facilitate environmental quality by limiting economic development . . . but how to create a system of production that can grow and develop in harmony with the environment."

A CONTINUING MISSION

1. AIO has worked with EPA since its inception and with its first administrator, Russell Train. AIO did the following: (1) helped to create the first Indian Desk during the Nixon administration; (2) was instrumental in drafting and institutionalizing the first American Indian policy statement adopted by a federal agency; (3) orchestrated an agreement between six federal agencies to work on a government-to-government basis with tribal governments on environmental issues; (4) held six regional meetings with tribes and developed *Messing with Mother Nature*, a publication that became the tribal handbook on how to deal with the federal government on environmental issues; (5) organized two forums with state governors and tribes to formalize state and tribal governmental relations with a special emphasis on environmental issues, with the cooperation of the Western Governors' Association; (6) hosted a national forum to initiate a mandate to organize a national Indian environmental protection organization; (7) worked with Council of Energy Resources Tribes and the Native American Rights Fund to build a foundation for the creation of a national environmental organization (the National Tribal Environment Council (NTEC); (8) contracted with EPA to hold four regional conferences to identify the barriers that tribal governments face in working cooperatively with the EPA and how to overcome these barriers; (9) published *Partners for the Protection of the Environment*,

a pamphlet summarizing these barriers and solutions; and (10) established INDIANet to help tribes access EPA Indian information electronically.

2. The W. K. Kellogg Foundation is a nonprofit organization whose stated mission is "to help people help themselves through the practical application of knowledge and resources to improve their quality of life and that of future generations."

3. From Alexander Pope's *Essay on Man*, line 99.

"Lo, the poor Indian! whose untutor'd mind
Sees God in the clouds, or hears him in the wind;
His soul proud Science never taught to stray
Far as the solar walk or milky way;
Yet simple nature to his hope has giv'n
Behind the cloud-topped hill, an humbler heav'n."

4. From the *Albuquerque Journal*, 3 April 1997: "Leadership Program Gets Boost. Kellogg Gives Indian Group $1 Million. Americans for Indian Opportunity has received over $1 million for 1997 from the W. K. Kellogg Foundation to support its national leadership training program for young Native American leaders. A Kellogg spokesman said the grant could total $3.3 million for three years if AIO can secure matching funds. [LaDonna] Harris said the 91 graduates of the program, which began in 1993, include Native American lawyers, doctors, educators, elected officials, fund-raisers, business owners and artists from more than 66 tribes. Harris said the Kellogg commitment will help AIO raise matching funds from private sources and other foundations. 'It should help them understand there are other ways to make positive changes, rather than just funding traditional Indian programs [that address] alcoholism and poverty,' Harris said."

INDEX

Adobe Walls, battle of, 5–7
Alaskan claims legislation, 91
Albert, Carl, 81, 88, 137 n.6
American Indian Movement (AIM), 94, 140 n.10
Americans for Indian Opportunity (AIO): Ambassadors Program, 121–23; creation of, 99, 141 n.3; first board of directors of, 103–4; fundraising for, 99–103; office of, xiv–xv; projects of, 109, 143 n.1; successes of and future plans for, 117–21
Anderson, Clinton, 88–90
Antelope Eaters (Quahadas), 4, 8

Brown, Ron, 82
Byrd, Harry, 92

Choctaws, and termination, 63, 135 n.9

Citizens' Party, 110, 111
Comanches: attitude toward death of, 107; and battle of Adobe Walls, 5–7; and battle of Palo Duro Canyon, 7–9; and breakaway from KCA, 48; at Fort Sill, 9; and help of Fred, 47; identification as, 132 n.13; LaDonna's wish for, 116; and Oklahomans for Indian Opportunity, 61; Quahada band of (Antelope Eaters), 4, 8; Toyah band of, xviii; values of, xviii–xix, 13, 34; Yamparika band of (Root Eaters), 4
Commoner, Barry, 110–11, 142 n.2

Dawes Act, provisions of, 1–2
Deer, Ada, 63, 136 n.12

Edmondson, James Howard (Ed), 65–66,

Edmondson, James Howard (*cont.*) 81, 136–37 n.1

Eklund, Coy, 101–3

Equitable Life Insurance Company, 101

Evans, Billie Carl, 56, 17, 19, 26, 38

Fort Sill ok: 1874 incarceration of Quahadas at, 8; Indian hospital at, 18; Indian school at, 17; John Tabbytite stationed at, 9–10

Harris, Byron, 53, 134 n.4

Harris, Fred R.: and Alaskan claims legislation, 91; as candidate for governor, 65; and college and law school, 39–42; divorce and remarriage of, 112–14; as Future Farmers of America prizewinner, 32; and Hubert H. Humphrey, 86; as husband and father, 34, 36–37; and Kerner Commission, 84; law practice of, 45; and legislation for Taos Pueblo Indians, 90; and Lyndon B. Johnson, 68–69; meets and dates LaDonna, 28–29; and mental health committee, 54; entrance into politics of, 43; as an Oklahoma state senator, xiii, 50; as a presidential candidate, xiii, 105; and Tabbytites' oil and water problems, 44; and Univ. of New Mexico job offer, 110; as a U.S. Senator, xiii, 66–72; and work for Comanches, 47

Harris, Kathryn. See Tijerina, Kathryn Harris

Harris, LaDonna: as candidate for vice president, 110–12; on death, 107–8; descriptions of family members by, 17–18, 23–26; on discrimination, 62, 66; divorce of, 112–13, 114; and farm chores, 15; first home of, 38; and Fred's campaign for president, 105; and Fred's campaign for state senate, 50, 52–53; and Fred's campaign for U.S. Senate, 66–72; as Fred's helpmate in school, 40–42; girlhood games of, 13–15; heritage and relatives of, 3–11; jobs held by, 39–40; and Lawton society, 49, 54, 55–56; marriage and pregnancy of, 34, 35–37; meets and dates Fred, 28–29; as mental health committee member, 75–78, 83; move to New Mexico of, 110; personal philosophy of, 61; self-consciousness in public of, 58–59; and study of Indian drop-out rates, 59; teenage social life of, 26–28, 31–33; and view of contemporary Native American situation, 117–25; and the Washington dc social scene, 79

Harris, Laura, xx; birth of, 68; as a child, 92–94; as an employee of Americans for Indian Opportunity, xiv–xv; marriage of, 115; and son, Sam Fred, 115

Health, Education and Welfare (hew), mental health committee of, 75–78, 83

Honcho Group, 55–56, 58

Humphrey, Hubert H., 71–72, 85–86

Jackson, Scoop, 88–89

Johnson, Lyndon B., 68–69, 84–85

Kennedy, Robert, and family, 72–73, 74

Kerner Commission, 84, 87, 138 n.1

Kerr, Robert S., 66, 137 n.2

Lawton Junior League, 49

Lawton ok, 49, 54, 56

Menominees, and termination, 63, 91, 136 n.11

Mondale, Walter F., 85, 99, 137 n.4

Monroney, A. S. "Mike," 68, 137 n.3

Muskie, Edward, 86–87

National Congress of American Indians
(NCAI), 99, 141 n.12
National Indian Opportunities Council,
81; hearings of, 95–98
Native American Rights Fund (NARF), 10
Nixon, Richard M., 89–90, 95

Office of Economic Opportunity (OEO),
73–74, 78
Ojibwes, 102, 142 n.2; relocation of, 91–92
Oklahomans for Indian Opportunity
(OIO): book donations of, 61–62; and
Choctaw termination, 63; establishment
of, 59; funding for, 78; purpose of, 135
n.5; study of Indian drop-out rates, 59

Palo Duro Canyon, battle of, 7–8
Parker, Quanah (Comanche chief),
128–29 n.5; family connection to, 10–11
peyote, 20, 24
polygamy, Comanche practice of, 132 n.12

Quahadas (Antelope Eaters), 4, 8

religion, 19–22
Root Eaters (Yamparikas), 4

Shinnecocks, 100, 141 n.1
Shriver, Sarge, 73, 78, 80
Southwest Center for Human Relations
Studies (Univ. of Oklahoma): and
the Bureau of Indian Affairs, 57;
Comanche participation in, 58; focus

on Indian education of, 57; LaDonna's
introduction to, 56

Tabbytite, John (grandfather): farm of,
xiii, xx, 2, 13, 16; at home, 23; personal
history of, 4; personality of, 24; on
Quanah Parker, 11; religious beliefs of,
20, 24; as a soldier at Fort Sill, 9–10
Tabbytite, Lily (mother): death of, 107;
employee of Fort Sill Indian hospital,
18, 63; as a student at Fort Sill Indian
school, 17
Tabbytite, Wick-ie (grandmother):
attendance at Kathryn's wedding of, 107;
death of, 107; as farm wife, 15–17; and
Fred's campaign, 67–68; religious beliefs
of, 20; in Washington DC, 130 n.3
Tabbytite Henderson, Rose Marie (aunt),
14, 16–17, 19, 21, 25, 28
Taos Blue Lake, 88
Taos Pueblo, legislation to protect, 88, 89,
90, 139–40 n.4
Tijerina, Kathryn Harris: and antiwar
movement, 85–86; attitude toward law
enforcement of, 132 n.1; birth of, 36;
marriage of, 106; political beliefs of, 92;
professional life of, 133 n.3
Toyahs, mission statement of, xviii

Udall, Stewart, 78

War on Poverty program, 81, 88

Yamparikas (Root Eaters), 4

I Tell You Now
Autobiographical Essays by
Native American Writers
Edited by Brian Swann and
Arnold Krupat

Postindian Conversations
By Gerald Vizenor and
A. Robert Lee

Chainbreaker
The Revolutionary War Memoirs of
Governor Blacksnake
As Told to Benjamin Williams
Edited by Thomas S. Abler

Standing in the Light
A Lakota Way of Seeing
By Severt Young Bear and R. D. Theisz